CPAs THAT SELL

A Complete Guide
to Promoting Your
Professional Services

CPAs THAT SELL
A Complete Guide to Promoting Your Professional Services

August J. Aquila, Ph.D.

Allan D. Koltin, CPA

Robert Pitts, Ph.D.

IRWIN
Professional Publishing
Chicago • Bogatá • Boston • Buenos Aires • Caracas
London • Madrid • Mexico City • Sydney • Toronto

Irwin Professional Book Team

Executive editor: *Amy Hollands Gaber*
Acquistions editor: *Amy Ost*
Marketing manager: *Brian Hayes*
Production supervisor: *Laurie Kersch*
Assistant manager, desktop services: *Jon Christopher*
Project editor: *Denise Santor-Mitzit*
Designer: *Matthew Baldwin*
Compositor: *Douglas & Gayle, Ltd.*
Typeface: *11/13 Times Roman*
Printer: *Quebecor Book Press*

Times Mirror
Higher Education Group

Library of Congress Cataloging-in-Publication Data

Aquila, August J.
    CPAs that sell: a complete guide to promoting your professional
services/August J. Aquila, Allan D. Koltin, Robert Pitts.
        p. cm.
    Includes index.
    ISBN 0-7863-0196-1
    1. Accounting—Marketing. I. Koltin, Allan D. II. Pitts, Robert
A. III. Title.
HF5657.A67 1996
657'.068'8—dc20   95–21706

For Emily Haliziw-Aquila, Sharon Koltin,
and Cheryl Pitts, you are the best part of us.

The American Institute of Certified Public Accountants (AICPA) is the national professional organization for all Certified Public Accountants. The mission of the AICPA is to act on behalf of its members and provide necessary support to assure that CPAs serve the public interest in performing the highest quality of professional services. In fulfilling its mission, the AICPA gives priority to those areas where public reliance on CPA skills is most significant.

Practice Development Institute (PDI) is a management and marketing consulting firm that specializes in helping professional service firms achieve greater growth and profits. PDI has provided training, consulting, and products to over 10,000 CPA firms throughout greater North America.

Introduction

When the idea for this book first came about, we knew that it would be a challenge to capture the key elements for showing you how to become a successful new business development expert. There was so much to say, and we were confined to a set number of pages. We wanted the book to be read above all else, and we wanted you to be more efficient in business development when you finished reading and working through the exercises in this book. That's why the layout is different from most selling books that you might have read in the past.

We decided to start each chapter with a self-assessment. These are meant to give you some idea of what you know or don't know about the topic covered in the chapter. In addition, they are meant to get you thinking about the way you currently develop new business. Knowledge is important, but more important is the ability to do something with it. Perhaps most important is your belief that you can do it.

We are also trying to teach you a process: how to develop new business. This is not a strictly linear process, but our explanation of the process has to be linear. We have tried to explain what to do first, second, third, and so on, although things every seldom happen like this in the real world. So we ask you to bear with us as we go through the selling cycle.

The following is a conversation the likes of which is being heard in accounting firms throughout the country on an almost daily basis. There are two speakers. The senior partner (SP), in his early sixties, is a successful practice developer. The young associate (YA) is trying to find out how he or she can become a partner in the firm. Let's cut into the middle of their conversation.

YA: "How am I ever going to make partner in this firm? What do I have to do to make sure I achieve this goal?"

SP: "Let's assume the other partners recognize your technical skills, and there are no real personality conflicts. The most important factor in

	your becoming a partner here is purely economic. In other words, how much business can you bring to the partnership so we can continue to grow and ultimately bring in more partners?"
YA:	"That's all it takes to become a partner?"
SP:	"Yes, but it's easier said than done. My experience has shown me there aren't a lot of accountants who know how to bring in business. It's easy for us to find CPAs with excellent technical skills, but when it comes to practice development and great client handling skills, it's a lot harder."
YA:	"Skills?" I always thought people were born with great marketing personalities and selling abilities. Are you telling me I can learn them?"
SP:	"Not only can you learn them, you *need* to learn them if you want to eventually become a partner here. And I'm going to show you how. It won't happen overnight, but then you didn't become the tax expert you are today overnight either. So be patient and work at developing the skills I'm going to share with you. I know you can do it. I started doing it 30 years ago when I was in your shoes, and I'm still learning. I found out long ago that selling our services is a continuous process that never ends. So let's start now with your first lesson."

If this conversation sounds familiar to you or if you have been searching for a way to learn how to develop business, then you will want to read and reread this book. Depending on your current skill level, you probably won't have to read the entire book. As we said, each chapter starts with a self-assessment to help you identify areas that you need to work on. So before you begin a chapter, take the self-assessment. Also, remember the following questions as you read this book:

1. How can I put what I am reading to use right now?
2. How should I change my current way of doing business development to become more efficient?
3. How should I be changing my current way of thinking about selling my firm's professional services?
4. How will what I am reading help me to better service my clients?

We will continuously remind you of these questions as we progress through the chapters.

This book would not have been possible without the help of many successful accountants and consultants in the country. Over the past 16 years, we have had the opportunity to work with many of them and to listen to their stories of success and failure. We could not begin to mention all of them. There are, however, a few we would like to pay particular thanks: David Cottle, Tom Feeley, Barry Friedman, Irwin Friedman, Harvey Goldstein, John Hamilton, Don Istvan, Charlie Larson, Mike McCaffrey, Jay Nisberg, and Howard Schnoll. There are countless others who have helped us, listened to us, and even counseled us. You know who you are, and we can only say "Thanks." We are also grateful to the AICPA's Management of an Accounting Practice Committee for their invaluable review of the manuscript. Finally, we want to thank Amy H. Gaber, executive editor and Patrick Muller, development editor at Irwin Professional Publishing, and Pam Sourelis, our copy editor, who provided the necessary structure and critical review of the manuscript.

August J. Aquila, Ph.D.
Allan D. Koltin, CPA
Robert Pitts, Ph.D.

Minneapolis and Chicago, 1995

The following are the members of the AICPA Management of an Accounting Practice Committee Task Force who provided reviews of this book:

J. Frank Betts, Jr., CPA
Eurbank & Betts
Jackson, Mississippi

Robert H. Given, CPA
Given & Company
Santa Monica, California

J. Vern Williams, CPA
Williams, Cox, Weidner & Cox
Tallahassee, Florida

Table of Contents

Chapter One

What They Never Told You in B School

"Nothing sells a professional service better than a professional"

Anonymous

INTRODUCTION

Business schools have done a fantastic job teaching future accountants a great deal about accounting principles, finance, and taxes. What they haven't taught accountants is the importance of building their practice or—to use a word that often brings chills to the accountant's spine—"sales." Unfortunately, accountants have had to learn about the selling of professional services through the school of hard knocks. Many accountants have never learned the importance of selling their services or developed the skills needed to be successful at it. We know through our experiences that it is not unusual for accountants to feel uneasy when it comes to "selling" their services.

We have consulted with thousands of accountants, from sole practitioners to partners in some of the largest firms, and have noticed that many accountants either have a negative attitude toward the word *sales* and the concept of "selling something" or are downright afraid of it. This chapter will change your negative attitudes and put your fears to rest once and for all. We will show you that the most successful accountants are also the best "salespeople" in their firms. They see themselves as problem solvers for their clients. They measure their success not only by the number of new clients they acquire but also by their clients' satisfaction with their services. Finally, these accountants are successful because they have developed the skills needed to effectively communicate and build a true partnership with their clients.

Before you begin to read this chapter, take the following two self-assessments. They will give you some idea of how much you already know about selling accounting services.

SELF ASSESSMENT 1–1: WHAT'S YOUR ATTITUDE TOWARD SELLING ACCOUNTING SERVICES?

Take a minute and answer each of the following questions as truthfully as possible:

1. Clients are only interested in the lowest price they can get. True or false?
2. Selling is not really a professional activity. True or false?
3. There is no difference between selling a product and selling a professional service. True or false?
4. I could never learn how to be an effective seller of professional services. True or false?
5. Your goal in a sales situation is to seek win–lose relationships with your clients. True or false?

If you answered "false" to all of these questions, you should probably go on to the next chapter. You have an excellent understanding of the basic concepts of selling professional services. However, for each question that you responded "true," you will need to do some additional homework and read this chapter.

The next assessment will give you an idea of what characteristics you need to be successful at selling your services.

SELF ASSESSMENT 1–2: HOW DO YOU RATE AS A SELLER OF PROFESSIONAL SERVICES?

Which of the following characteristics do you possess? I have (am):

	Yes	No
1. Extremely aggressive personality		
2. Strong verbal skills		
3. Strong listening skills		

4. Overly friendly
5. Manipulative
6. Above-average intelligence
7. High degree of self-confidence
8. High degree of drive
9. Pressured buyers into decisions
10. Good analytical problem-solving skills
11. Knowledgeable about handling objections
12. Knowledgeable about closing
13. High degree of product/technical knowledge
14. Good at accepting rejection

Now for the answers:

Most accountants already possess the characteristics found in numbers 6, 7, 8, 10, and 13. It takes a lot of intelligence to pass the CPA exam, have your own practice, and work in a profession that has a tremendous amount of pressure and requires a high degree of drive. Good analytical problem-solving is something most of you feel very comfortable doing, and you know you are good at it. Keeping up to date with the myriad of tax law changes and accounting updates provides you with outstanding product knowledge. All outstanding salespeople know their products and services inside and out.

You might be weak in areas 2, 3, 11, 12, and 14. Again, outstanding salespeople excel in these areas. These are all skills that you can learn and are topics that we will discuss in future chapters. With a little practice and training, you will feel quite comfortable in these areas.

Characteristics 1, 4, 5, and 9 are all negative. If you checked any of these, you will want to do some reverse learning. These are the characteristics and attitudes toward selling that give salespeople and selling a bad reputation.

WHY PERSONAL SALES?

Why do we have personal sales in an age of mass media, databases, advertising, telecommunications, and direct marketing? Why should I, a highly skilled accountant, spend my time selling when my expertise is in accounting, taxes, and business consulting, not selling or marketing?

Selling, so the current accounting paradigm tells us, takes the professional away from the job he or she selected and was trained for. It
takes the accountant outside of his or her skills and knowledge base.
And the time spent selling is not billable! We know what is running
through the minds of the accountants: "What if I am not successful at
this activity? What will I have to show for my time?"

This is also an important issue in today's cost-conscious, production-
oriented, and accountability centered environment. First, personal selling is very expensive. According to the "1993 Sales Management's
Budget Planner" in the authoritative *Sales and Marketing Management*
magazine (June 28, 1993) selling expenses run almost 11 percent of
total sales in consumer goods and industrial firms and a whopping 15
percent plus in service firms. By comparison, advertising and promotion expenses are only 4.5, 3.0, and 3.4 percent respectively in these
industries. The median cost of a single sales call in service industries
was $213.64 in 1992. In the accounting profession, the cost of a sales
call (i.e., "the opportunity cost," meeting the prospect, preparing a
proposal, presenting your proposal, etc.) can range from several hun-
dred to thousands of dollars. Second, there is tremendous pressure on
partners and accountants in general to be highly productive—either being
highly billable or bringing in a lot of new business. If you spend a lot
of time marketing and selling, there is *no* guarantee you will bring in
new business.

Despite the costs and the risks involved, the answers to Why sell?
are really quite simple. While personal selling is very expensive, nothing communicates—solves client problems—like one-on-one/eye-to-eye
communication. And nothing sells professional services like the professional who provides them. While selling is expensive and risky, you
need to have clients to stay in business. Personal selling is the key to
building your practice.

"PERSONAL SELLING" DEFINED

Before we move ahead, let's define what we mean by personal selling
of accounting services.

> Personal selling of accounting services is the process of solving client prob-
> lems by satisfying their needs with your firm's services and products through
> a process of interpersonal communication.

This definition is based on the idea that any business or profession exists solely to satisfy the needs of its customers by providing the proper services. For accountants, these services encompass a wide range, from traditional accounting and tax compliance to specialized consulting services. It has often been said that accountants today are in the business of solving their clients' problems, no matter what those problems are.

As business school students, you were exposed to Maslow's hierarchy of needs. Maslow, you will recall, tells us that our needs range from the very basic needs of food and shelter to the higher and more complex needs of self-esteem and love. At some level, literally everything we or our clients do can be explained as being directed toward the satisfaction of one or more of these fundamental needs. Needs that are left unfulfilled will cause a certain amount of dissatisfaction in our lives.

The same is true for the business owner, manager, or anyone who is trying to satisfy a need. For example, one of your clients may need to develop a system that will help them better track their inventory. As a professional, you will first need to identify that need and then come up with a workable and affordable solution. If you can do this, you have solved your client's problem and will undoubtedly be able to sell your solution. Successful personal selling is simply about the process of satisfying a client's needs by solving the problem at hand. In a recent issue of *Fortune* magazine (July 25, 1994), the following headline appeared: "Today's customers want solutions, and companies are remaking their sales forces to satisfy them."

Let's look at the following example:

A client we know once wanted to buy a point-of-sales system that would make his small retail operations run more efficiently and profitably. He was looking for a point-of-sales system that would allow him to track his inventory and tie sales right into his general ledger. When we met him, several other accountants had already approached him with their products and solutions but were unable to get him to say yes. When we asked him why he was still trying to solve his problem, he told us that the other vendors were selling him a product, not a solution. The products they proposed were either too expensive or too complex or just didn't meet the needs of this business owner. His needs were simple; he didn't want to spend an arm and a leg. He also wanted to feel that the people he was going to work with would be able to train him and his employees on the new system. It took three meetings in all to uncover all his needs and concerns. By using the skills and concepts we will present in this book, we were able to obtain this prospect as a new client.

The successful accountants we know see themselves as problem solvers. That's why they are successful. But to solve problems, you need to be able to identify needs and communicate effective solutions to your clients. Much more will be said about this throughout this book. For now, just remember:

Needs identification will be the basis of your ultimate success.

SELLING IS A MULTISTEP PROCESS

Personal selling is the link between the firm and the client. Yet our experience has been that most accounting firms and accountants are struggling to become effective at personal selling. Intellectually, they all realize the importance of doing it. Accountants have told us, "It's a matter of life and death." But the majority of accountants are finding that becoming more proficient in personal selling is much more difficult to accomplish than acquiring more technical accounting and tax skills. We won't try to kid you; you will need to work long and hard to become proficient in personal selling. It's no different than the time you spent becoming a proficient accountant, tax advisor, or consultant.

Most accountants also fail to realize that selling their services is a multistep process. Unless you were fortunate to have a sales course in business school, you, like most other accountants, want to jump to the end of the process rather than taking it step-by-step. To be successful, you need to view personal selling and selling activities in your firm as a continuous multistep process. This process involves developing opportunities; setting up appointments with prospects; planning your sales call; creating credibility with the prospect; probing in order to identify concerns, real or imaginary; developing solutions to those concerns; overcoming objections; justifying your costs; getting the client to say yes; and keeping the client for life.

BUILDING A SALES CULTURE

In *Bankers Who Sell: Improving Selling Effectiveness in Banking,* Leonard L. Berry, Charles M. Futrell, and Michael R. Bowers outline the success factors in the sales process. They refer to these sales success factors as the Sales Loop Model (Figure 1–1) and break the model down into nine distinct activities. What Berry and the other authors learned was "No magic answer or easy approach to a successful sales program is available....The elements are ongoing rather than discrete. That is, they require continuous development and refinement and attention." (p. 32)

We feel that these nine critical success factors are as appropriate for the accounting industry as the banking/financial services industry. In fact, the first one, building a sales culture, is at the crux of whether a firm will have a successful sales program. We have found that accountants' negative attitudes toward selling may be one of the biggest obstacles to effectively selling accounting services. Unlike those who enter the financial services industry (insurance, banking, personal financial planning, etc.), those who enter the accounting profession never expect to have to sell. And for a long time, they did not have to.

In the 1970s and 1980s, the typical accountant could just be an order taker. To be successful 10 or 20 years ago, an accountant did not have to worry about building a sales culture, employing professionals who could also sell, developing creative sales techniques, or being client centered. During a large part of the 1980s, marketing and new business development was understood to be a promotion-based activity—newsletters, seminars, public relations, institutional advertising, and so on. To a great degree, personal selling was still not required.

This can be easily explained. For most of the 1970s and 1980s, demand for accountants' services was greater than supply. Hence, the accounting industry did not find itself in a personal sales environment. The realities of the 1990s in the accounting profession have changed all this. The supply of accountants far exceeds the demand for their services. Clients are more sophisticated than ever before; and through the use of PCs, clients can perform many, if not most, of the basic accounting and tax functions that only an accountant knew how to do before. Accountants can no longer just be "order takers." The new environment calls for a professional who is truly trained in identifying

FIGURE 1–1
Sales Success Factors

1. Building a sales culture.
2. Defining the sales task.
3. Having the right people sell.
4. Having the right services to sell.
5. Preparing people to sell.
6. Facilitating selling.
7. Measuring selling performance.
8. Rewarding selling performance.
9. Developing sales managers.

Source: Barry, Leonard L, et al. *Bankers Who Sell.* Burr Ridge Il, Irwin Professional Publishing, 1985, p. 32.

client needs and who knows how to satisfy them. In short, the new environment calls for an "order getter." This environment requires a completely different set of personal and technical skills, a new attitude toward selling, and a new selling approach.

Although there is a great deal of talk about accounting firms becoming more sales oriented and building a sales culture, we have found that most firms are moving very slowly toward a true sales culture. Firms that have embraced the sales culture usually show the following characteristics:

1. The most important characteristic is to be **client centered.** Successful firms have had this characteristic for some time. For these firms, clients were often defined as internal as well as external clients. Above all, clients are put first in the firm. A managing partner once told us that his partners did not have quotas and, above all, did not pressure existing clients to purchase additional services; rather, the emphasis was on client needs. "The more we focused on needs," he said, "the more new business came in. Believe it or not, it was that simple."

2. Accounting firms that truly create a sales orientation have developed a **team approach.** These firms don't have salespeople, but they do have industry teams. Accountants who work on teams find that they gain strength from their fellow team members. They don't feel alone in the business development process.

3. **Top management supports** 110 percent the sales orientation in work and deed. They participate in all marketing programs and

are often the leaders. They lead by deed rather than by dictum. The way senior partners and management spend their time, what they support, and how they act is paramount in the development of the proper culture.

4. There is a **strong sense of firm.** Those firms that have a strong sales orientation have a strong firm orientation. The firm may have a long tradition or a strong position in the marketplace. The partners and the staff exhibit a certain pride in being part of the firm. The standards and expectations of quality and service at these firms are also higher than at the average firm. The clients are clients of the firm not of any one individual partner.

5. The firm provides for their partners and staff the necessary **training, encouragement, and rewards.** Firm management shows that they have confidence in the ability of their professionals to develop new skills and that under the right circumstances these professionals will embrace the new culture. Management style in these firms is supportive; it looks to building teams and strong individuals within those teams.

In today's environment, every professional needs to realize that a sales orientation is part of business and a critical part of a professional role. Part of that role is ultimately asking prospects, referral sources, and existing clients for business. Too often we fail to obtain a new engagement because we just don't ask for it. The worst that can happen when you ask is that someone says no. But the consultative partnership approach that we will teach you is designed to minimize the number of no's you will hear. By working like a consultant and establishing a relationship that works like a business partnership, you will hear a lot more yeses. You will learn that true selling in today's professional environment is based on the client's need satisfaction not the trickery or flimflam often associated with old-style selling.

SO WHAT'S STOPPING YOU?

If selling and a sales orientation is so important, what keeps some people from being sales oriented? Maybe they just don't feel they have what it takes to be sales oriented.

There is some evidence that physically attractive salespeople are more effective, but we don't know that super salesperson Ross Perot was ever accused of being pretty. The real obstacles to your success in selling accounting services are not how you look but how you think and how you work at selling. Your fear of selling is your biggest obstacle. We have found that if you can put your fears down in writing, they become less of an obstacle because you get them out of your mind and start to do something positive to overcome them.

Take two more minutes and answer the question in Figure 1–2.

Our consulting experience with numerous firms and literally thousands of accountants indicates that you probably listed several of the following reasons.

1. **It's not my job.** Then whose job is it? Let us assure you that nobody can sell professional services like the professional.
2. **I don't have a good understanding of all the services that my firm provides.** You need to gain this knowledge if you are to effectively serve your clients and be effective as a member of your firm.
3. **I don't know how to ask for the business.** We will show you how in this book.
4. **I don't know where to find clients.** We will show you in this book.
5. **No one ever told me to do it.** You only need to sell your services in today's accounting environment if you want to make and stay a partner in your firm. If you don't, some other aggressive accountant will.
6. **I don't have to do it; I'm a partner now.** What counts in most firms today is the ability to bring in business. You can no longer bet your future on technical skills alone.
7. **We don't have accountability here; we're all friends.** This will work as long as the firm is making money. It won't be the same when revenues start to decline. Trust us.

Please allow us to add one additional item to the list that many accountants won't admit to themselves but which is one of the basic barriers to being successful at bringing in new business:

Selling is scary. What if I fail? If my client says no to me, will I lose face with the person?

Fear of rejection is in fact the primary fear, the main negative attitude that keeps many accountants from ever being effective at developing business for their firm. Many people are not sales oriented because

FIGURE 1–2
What are the key barriers that prevent you from getting started?

1. _____
2. _____
3. _____
4. _____
5. _____

selling inherently seems to mean that you are going to have to endure rejection. A typical salesperson makes about four calls per day, of which only one may actually produce a sale. This can be viewed as one rewarding experience in four but often is viewed as three punishing experiences in four. A good salesperson lives for the reward of success, but for many of us the rejection is simply too much to endure. Thus, one of the key characteristics that many contend is important for a professional salesperson is drive and enthusiasm so that one can be thick-skinned and endure rejection. To be effective in sales, you must always keep your spirit and enthusiasm up for the win. We will show you how to feel good about selling.

SUMMARY

Let's face it, we have all had negative experiences with certain types of salespeople and sales environments. Receiving cold calls from salespeople during a busy day or at dinner does little to give anyone a positive opinion of sales activities. Buying a car is one of the largest purchases most of us make. Yet, very few car buyers have had a positive experience in what is frequently a bargaining trial by fire, one in which few will ever really beat the seller. Yes, there is a mental hurdle to overcome. It all boils down to this: *Selling is important.* And it can be done in a professional manner. As firms begin to offer their clients more complex services, only the professional who can articulate the benefits of these services, clarify for the client what he or she will re-ceive, provide alternative solutions to business problems, and develop a client relationship of trust will succeed and prosper.

Relationship building requires satisfying the client's total business needs, not just a small portion of them. No one, and we mean no one, can do this except the professional accountant and consultant.

The consultative partnership approach we will show you in the next chapter eliminates many of the barriers for the accounting professional who must be sales oriented in today's environment.

Chapter Two

The Consultative Partnership Approach (*CPA*): All You Really Need to Know About Selling

INTRODUCTION

This chapter will teach you all you really need to know about the process of buying and selling. The Consultative Partnership Approach (*CPA*) for selling accounting services is based on three key principles. In this chapter, we will explain each of the elements of the *CPA* method in simple constructs you can use as the foundation of your approach to selling your firm's services. To make this foundation even more concrete, we will discuss the results of our survey of accountants who apply these concepts in their own practices. As you read and work though the chapter, you will learn how to analyze why and how decisions are made by prospects and clients and how to apply our Consultative Partnership Approach to selling accounting and consulting services.

Before you begin reading this chapter, take Self-Assessment 2–1 to find out how much you really know about the prospect decision cycle (i.e., the buying cycle).

SELF ASSESSMENT 2–1: PROSPECT/CLIENT ANALYSIS EXERCISE

Pick either one of your most important clients that you think you know the best or a current prospect that you soon plan to ask for their business. Then complete the following client analysis form.

Client/prospect name: _____

Current relationship: _____

List here the prospect/client needs you have identified: _____

_____

_____

_____

_____

List the potential service offerings you have identified: _____

_____

_____

_____

_____

List the benefits that your services will provide: _____

_____

_____

_____

_____

Describe how each of the following (gatekeepers, users, influencers, buyers, and deciders) were involved in the purchase decision process:

1. Problem recognition
2. Need description
3. Information search
4. Product specification
5. Evaluation of alternatives
6. Vendor search
7. Vendor selection
8. Purchase decision
9. Performance review
10. Post-purchase behavior

Who are the gatekeepers in the organization?

Name: _____

Title: _____

Name: _____

Title: _____

Do you know the real users of the service?

Name: _____

Title: _____

Name: _____

Title: _____

Who has influence over the purchase decision?
Name: _____
Title: _____

Name: _____
Title: _____

Who are the ultimate decision makers:
Name: _____
Title: _____

Name: _____
Title: _____

If you had difficulty filling out this self-assessment, don't worry. We will provide you with the knowledge to answer these questions by the time you finish reading this chapter.

SELLING THEORIES AND PRACTICES

It is necessary to understand some of the history of modern selling theory and practice in American business in order to gain insight into how you should approach selling in your firm. Below we identify three different approaches to selling and explain how accountants may view each one of them.

The Traditional Sales Approach: "I've got it; you will buy it."

The traditional approach to selling is oriented to giving the salesperson in a business situation the power necessary to close the sale. If your firm falls into this category, all that matters is making a sale. In other words, I've got it, and you *will* buy it. Accounting firms that embrace this attitude assume that profits will come mainly through volume. They look at their services as commodities and their clients as buyers, not really clients. This method works if you are selling low-end, commodity types of services and if the client is mainly concerned with price.

This approach, however, forgets one important element in the sales equation: the needs of the client. The traditional approach often is an adversarial struggle in which the salesperson must gain control to convince the buyer to buy. If you buy my product, I win and you lose. It would never appear to someone with this attitude that they would make an important sale without ever actually selling their product or service. Since they are not needs focused, they would not understand that simply letting a client know where to go to satisfy a need would be considered a successful sale. The traditional approach also emphasizes aggressive combative closing as the key to sales effectiveness.

This is the approach to selling that is generally perceived as undesirable by many in our society and tags anyone one who sells as suspect by many. Many accounting and tax professionals as well as the general public think that being sales oriented means being pushy and overly aggressive. So it's not unusual for an accountant to have negative feelings about selling something to his or her client. Our survey confirmed this. When we asked accountants to explain their feelings about selling in general and about selling their services, here is what they said:

- "Selling in general is a low status job."
- "Anybody can get a sales job, so a person in my position should not be 'selling'."
- "I didn't go to a top-notch school of accountancy just to sell."
- "I'm a partner now. Why should I have to do this?"

Unfortunately, accountants aren't the only ones who have such a negative orientation about salespeople and selling. This feeling is part of our popular culture. There are endless examples from movies and books. Let's look at a few of these. In the 1950's hit, *The Music Man,* a slick salesman sells the whole town on the idea of a band so he can sell musical instruments. Arthur Miller's *Death of a Salesman* made the trials of Willy Loman, the failing salesman, part of our contemporary culture. *Used Cars* is a black comedy about the tricks of the car sales business. In *Cadillac Man,* another car salesman tries to sell a widow a car at her husband's funeral. *Tin Men* shows every sleazy trick of the siding sales business. The movie *Wall Street* did little to glorify the stock brokerage business. The more recent movie *Glen Gary/ Glen Ross* looks at land sales as salesmen respond to badgering and abusive superiors by tricking and badgering customers into buying worthless land. Selling has fared little better on television, where shoe salesman Al Bundy provides fodder for every selling joke ever known. When was the last time you saw a movie that glorified a salesperson who solved his or her clients' problems? We don't think you will ever see one although that is what proficient and successful salespeople do all day long.

Why is selling frequently vilified? It's not because a good salesperson isn't well paid. *Sales and Marketing Magazine* reports that in 1993 the average compensation (salary, commission, and bonus) of a top-level salesperson was in excess of $65,000. Many stock brokers and financial planners make well over several hundred thousand dollars per year. Sales is viewed negatively because of the pressure placed on salespeople to get the sale at all costs. This results in many sales personnel stooping to any trick to make a sale. And this is exactly what stops most accountants from thinking that sales can be a professional activity.

A Customer Needs Approach: Creative Selling

Modern selling in reputable companies and particularly in the selling of professional services is as far from the characters we described in the "traditional" selling examples as possible. Successful accounting firms today understand that clients do not want to be defeated in a buying situation. Clients want a nonadversarial environment in which to make their purchase decisions and respond to a sales approach that emphasizes the buyers' not the sellers' needs. We mentioned the negative response most of us have had to buying a car. Consider the response some car companies, such as Saturn, have had to the consumers' dissatisfaction with the traditional approach to selling automobiles. The Saturn division of General Motors changed their entire approach to selling their product. They employ a no-price-negotiation strategy in an attempt to make the purchase nonadversarial and advertise that you will find nonaggressive sales personnel in their showrooms who care about the buyers' needs, not their commission.

In fact, the creative selling approach (i.e, focus on customer needs) has a long history. Most modern selling authorities have adopted some form of the customer needs model of selling identified by Edward K. Strong in 1925. (*The Psychology of Selling and Advertising,* New York: McGraw Hill, 1925). This approach added the idea of "creative selling" and a focus on "customer needs" to the traditional "make them buy what you've got" approach. In the customer needs model of selling, the customer, not the salesperson, has the power in the transaction, and the salesperson attempts to please the customer.

Creative selling was the technique through which the salesperson looked for ways in which the firm's products could satisfy the potential buyer's needs. Without the idea of creative selling, many firms were stuck between their rejection of the traditional hard sell and a passive order-taking mentality. Creative selling allows the firm to be much more aggressive in seeking business but focuses attention on the customer's needs, not the firm's products. To implement creative selling, many accounting firms have been required to institute extensive training programs. They have taught their accountants how to better understand and probe to find customer needs. They have also educated their accountants and consultants to better understand their own product and service offerings so as to find an acceptable match. Most national accounting firms started training their accountants and consultants in this method in the late 1970s.

A Consultative Partnership Approach (CPA)

As good as the customer needs and creative selling approach sounds, there is a still better method for selling professional services in general and accounting services in particular. Our experience has firmly convinced us that the best approach to selling accounting services is a consultative approach. We have named our approach to selling accounting services the Consultative Partnership Approach or *CPA*. This approach is based on three key principles. To be successful in this method, accountants need to do the following:

1. Seek consultative relationships with clients as true business partners.
2. Use consultative selling skills to solve client problems.
3. Embrace a sales orientation as part of your professional role.

Consultative selling is at the opposite end of the spectrum from the traditional selling method. The accountant who uses the consultative approach will treat each prospect as unique.

Seek Consultative Relationships with Clients as True Business Partners.   The two key constructs here are the elements of partnership and relationship. The first foundation of our approach is that you are seeking to establish a long-term consultative partnership with prospects and existing clients as business partners. By partnership, we mean that you eventually learn a great deal about your prospect's business and eventually become part of your prospect's decision-making team. You do this by focusing on their needs. To consult means to exchange ideas, to provide insights, guidance, and ultimately solutions that will make your client more profits, improve operations, or merely provide peace of mind.

The idea of a relationship goes right along with the partnership concept. You are not looking for a one-time sale of aluminum siding or band instruments and then a fast train out of town. Rather, you are seeking to form a partnership that is developed over time and throughout the sales process. This partnership is built block by block as you continue to solve problems and provide solutions. Your long-term goal is to so satisfy your prospects and clients with your services that you will not only keep existing business but be able to provide an ever-expanding range of services. As you learn of new client needs, you can help with your expertise and your firm's portfolio of services. This mutual benefit forms the basis for a partnership between accountant and client and produces a satisfied client who is more than happy to pay your fees. Who wouldn't want to have a partner who would solve your business problems, increase your profitability, cut excessive overhead, and improve operations?

Partnerships only work when all members gain from the relationship. In other words, the relationship has to be a win-win. Relationships also only work if there is a sharing of power between the partners. Consultative selling is really a departure from either the "I'm in control; you will buy" mindset of the traditional sales approach or the frequently more passive approach many apply when the focus is only on the customer's needs. Our consultative approach requires a sharing of trust and power. And yes, there is the implicit assumption in consultative selling that your firm and your services will be the right solution for the client needs. In fact, we assume you will learn so much about the needs of all your clients that your firm will become more client centered.

Finally, the sales cycle and relationship building take time to develop. The traditional accountant is many times too impatient when it comes to developing relationships with potential clients. Unfortunately, too many accountants feel that if they can't bill for the hour spent marketing, the hour is not worth the effort. True, it is easier to measure the billable hour, but your firm will never grow unless you realize that one hour of prospecting may ultimately be worth several hours of billable time.

Using the *CPA* method with your clients builds the strongest type of partnership and credibility. Clients soon realize how important they are to you and the value of your services to them. They soon become cheerleaders for you and your firm. Your focus becomes the long-term relationship you can build with the client rather than convincing the client to buy a single service.

When we asked some of the participants in our survey about client relationships, here is what they said:

"We feel that we are providing much more than just an audit or tax return. Not only are we selling the firm, but we are also selling a long-term relationship. Our relationships with our clients expand into strong personal relationships. It's not unusual for our partners and staff to develop friendships with our clients. Many times, our clients will call us with a personal matter; it might have to do with a son or daughter, whether they should sell their house, etc."

Another respondent wrote: "My success is really dependent upon the success of my clients. As they grow, so does my practice. If this is not being a partner with someone, I don't know what is."

A sole practitioner once told us: "My clients involve me in every business decision that they make. We both have a lot at stake. They can go out of business, and I could lose a valuable client."

Firms that embrace the *CPA* method of selling frequently develop these types of relationships. The above quotes give you some idea of the extent to which firms carry out the consultative idea.

Use Consultative Selling Skills to Solve Client Problems. In order to develop the relationship and partnership, you will need to learn new skills or to better utilize those you already possess. Figure 2–1 lists the skills you will need to be successful in our *CPA* approach. We will discusss these skills in greater detail in future chapters.

Embrace a Sales Orientation as Part of Your Professional Role. Finally, our approach is aggressively sales oriented. This means that you must always display three characteristics. One, you must be assertive when it comes to making sales. You just can't sit back and wait for the telephone to ring. Two, you need to act with a sense of urgency. When a lead develops, you can't wait until next week or even the next day to follow up. Three, you need to seek new clients with confidence because you can do the best job of handling their needs. If

FIGURE 2–1
Consultative Selling Skills

Identifing opportunities
Probing
Listening effectively
Relating to various selling situations
Presenting your solutions
Overcoming and handling objections
Asking for business and getting it
Managing your own behavior

---

your attitude toward sales does not change, you will never be successful. Your attitude, whether positive or negative, and your level of confidence are not only perceived by the prospect but will eventually have an impact on the outcome of the sales call. And without new clients, you will eventually go out of business.

A true sales orientation today simply cannot be adversarial, as in the traditional sales approach. Clients have too many choices to find solutions to their problems. If your clients feel that all you are selling is a product, they will be concerned with just one thing: How much is it going to cost? The *CPA* method will show you how to determine clients' needs and then help them with solutions that will alleviate their concerns.

After reading Chapter 1, you know why some accountants are not more sales oriented. You also know that successful accountants have overcome the barriers and are extremely sales-oriented. In fact successful accountants are constantly selling as much as any designated sales person. Maybe more! Every successful person is sales oriented for his or her ideas. Just think of the following examples:

- Sam Walton was "just" a merchant who understood his customers.
- Ross Perot was a computer service salesman.
- Every president of the United States is constantly selling his programs to Congress and to the country.
- Arthur Andersen was once a sole practitioner.

In fact, every successful business and organization depends on a sales orientation or attitude. It's your attitude toward your firm, your services, and yourself. Try to think of one company or even one of your clients that would be where they are today if they did not have a positive sales orientation. If you believe that you are really helping your clients, then selling is good; but if you don't, then selling something to someone is obviously bad. Our survey also indicated that in successful accounting firms, every one in the firm is sales oriented, not just the professional staff. There is no denying that firms will only have revenue and make a profit if they have sales. Japanese firms frequently send office and plant employees to work as salespeople when sales are down rather than have layoffs. We don't know of any accounting firms that have done this yet.

Now that you have some idea of the principles on which the *CPA* method is based, we will look at three additional concepts that you need to understand in order to be successful at selling your services: (1) Buying and selling are processes, (2) Clients buy benefits, and (3) Not all buying decisions are the same. By becomming aware of these concepts, you will better understand why selling and relationship building take time and why that time has real value for your firm.

BUYING AND SELLING ARE PROCESSES

One of the reasons client relationships take time to develop is because both buying and selling are processes. These are the processes you need to bring together if you are to be effective in selling your services. Let's first look at the process from the buyer's viewpoint (the Decision Cycle) and then from the seller's side (the Sales Cycle) and see how they go together. Figure 2–2 outlines the steps in the decision cycle and ties them with the steps in the selling cycle (Figure 2–2).

The Decision Cycle: The Buyer's Process

Understanding what the buyer is going through will help you become more sensitive to his or her needs and ultimately help you close more business. The prospective client's buying process or cycle is a ten-step approach.

1. The process always begins with **problem recognition**. It may be as simple as a client knowing that an annual audit is necessary because it is mandated by the covenants of the loan

FIGURE 2–2

Decision Cycle: the Buyer's Process	Sales Cycle: the Seller's Process
1. Problem recognition	1. Lead generation/prospecting
2. Need description	2. Setting up the appointment
3. Information search	3. Fact-finding or "scoping
4. Product specification	the engagement"
5. Evaluation of alternatives	4. Presenting your
6. Vendor search	solutions
7. Vendor selection	5. Asking the prospect to buy
8. Purchase decision	6. Follow-up
9. Performance review	
10. Post-purchase behavior	

agreement, which triggers the identification of the need for an appropriate audit. Often, however, problem recognition is not so simple nor so clearly delineated. For example, tax problems may be understood by the prospective client only in terms of IRS inquiries. A wealthy client may not even be aware that she or he has a severe estate tax problem. Nothing really happens until the prospect becomes aware of an existing or pending problem. As consultants to business owners, you can often make prospects aware of the negative consequences that can befall their business and personal financial situation if they do not do the proper planning.

2. **Need description** is the second step in the buying process, in which the buyer begins to translate his or her problems into the need that you will eventually have to satisfy. Perhaps an excessive tax bill is the problem, which will be translated into the need for more intensive tax planning. Or your wealthy client may read an article about estate taxes in your firm's newsletter and call you to determine if she or he should be concerned.

3. **Information search** may be a very short step or may take a very long time. The amount of information the client will seek about alternatives to satisfy a need will generally vary. It depends on the importance and complexity of the need and whether the buyer has previous experience in making such purchases. An information search may involve many sources of

information: personal acquaintances and other professional service providers, such as a lawyer, banker, personal financial advisor, stock broker, another business owner, and so on; actual research by the buyer through printed information such as niche newsletters, firm capability brochures; a request for proposal; and so on. Many accountants often fail to see the value of a niche newsletter. Clients will often use such a newsletter in the information search step. Sure, it is hard to measure the direct impact of such a newsletter, but we are confident you can now see the result if **your** information is not in front of the potential client.

4. **Product specification** is an important step for many larger firms who issue requests for proposals or who have a very formal process for evaluating vendors. More and more clients today are requesting proposals from their professional advisors. Much of the increase in requests for proposals deals with the client's desire to obtain a fair price. But at the same time, it permits the bidding firms to demonstrate their understanding of the client problem and their approach to solving the problem. Regardless of the formality of the process, the buyer ultimately will develop some idea of what he or she believes is an adequate solution to his or her needs.

5. & 6. **Evaluation of alternatives and vendor search** are steps in which the buyer narrows the field of competing products and services and identifies providers. Our model indicates that vendor search comes after evaluation of alternatives, but actually these steps may occur together, or the search for vendors may precede the evaluation of alternative, products and services. The order really depends on the amount of differentiation between the products/services offered by the marketplace to satisfy the prospective buyer's needs.

7. **Vendor selection** is the step in which the buyer decides which competing firm will provide the product/service. But in today's complex market, vendor selection is often the beginning of specification and price negotiations that may last several days or sometimes even weeks.

8. **Purchase decision** is the actual step in which the prospect decides that your product/service and firm as specified are appropriate. This is usually the close of negotiation. At this stage in the process, you should have a signed engagement letter that outlines the scope of your work and how your fees will be determined.

9 & 10. **Performance review and post-purchase behavior** are as much steps in the process as was initial problem recognition. But these are steps that most accountants seem to forget. Once the purchase decision has been made, you must always expect that your performance will be reviewed. Many accounting firms use a client satisfaction survey to provide a mechanism for the client to review the firm's performance as both a way of further cementing the long-term relationship and to improve future work. Finally, post-purchase behavior includes both future engagements and the interactions of clients, both satisfied and dissatisfied, with other firms. Remember the information search step above. Many, perhaps most, prospective clients gain information about your firm from current clients. Dissatisfied clients may be very vocal with their friends and acquaintances. Satisfied customers are, and always will be, your best source of promotion.

The Sales Cycle: The Seller's Process

Now let's look at the selling cycle or process. The buyer needs to go through a ten-step process to come to some decision, while the seller needs to go through a six-step process (see Figure 2–2) to ultimately make the sale. Once you understand the basics of the selling process, you will be on your way to closing more new business.

1. **Lead generation/prospecting** is the first step in selling. You have to identify prospective clients before you can begin to develop the relationship and satisfy their needs. As you will soon learn, it is very easy today to get a single address or phone number. In fact, you can easily access over 11 million business addresses and phone numbers. Lead generation and prospecting are processes thorough which you will identify and contact those firms with the greatest likelihood of becoming clients for your firm.

2. **Setting up the initial appointment** is the next step in the selling process. This is where you must gain the first true commitment of the prospective buyer. It may also be the first time you will actually make personal contact with the prospective client. You must use this step in the process to learn about the customer, to discover some basic needs, and to establish your position in the relationship.

3. **Fact-finding, or "scoping the engagement"** is normally the primary purpose of the first face-to-face meeting between the buyer and the seller. In this stage, you need to learn about your prospect's needs, about the business and people you will be working to serve. This is the very heart and soul of the *CPA* method and the basis for your relationship with your client. By identifying needs, you will have the information you need to determine the benefits you will be selling to the prospect. The identification of needs may actually begin at the very first contact with the prospect. However, it is the real reason for the fact-finding call.

4. **Presentation of your solutions** is a step in which you show how your products and services will satisfy the client's needs and solve the client's problem. This may either be a written proposal or an oral presentation to the prospect. It is in this step that you can relate features to benefits. Now also is the time to define your services in the context necessary to address the needs that the prospect seeks to satisfy. Much of the real selling job is the demonstration of how your services provide the benefits that will satisfy your client's needs.

   During this step, you will have to make adjustments with the prospect. This is the part of the *CPA* method that differentiates what you will be doing to serve a prospect's needs as a partner from what many consider to be old-style sales. You will often need to modify some part of your service to make it best satisfy an individual prospect. For example, a prospect is interested in doing a profit improvement review of his entire operation. You estimate there will be about 50 hours of effort; at your standard billing rate of $150, the total fee will be $7,500. The prospect isn't totally sure of the benefit of this profit improvement review. You might suggest that only a segment of the business be reviewed at a much lower cost. If the client is satisfied, you would complete the engagement. Or you could tell the client that if he does not receive value for the services you provide, he has the option of paying you only for the perceived value.

5. **Asking the prospect to buy** is considered by many as the key to selling. We feel if you have gone through the consultative partnership approach correctly, you will find that closing is really quite simple. You have presented your solution to the client's current problem, have developed a relationship,

and are beginning to partner with the prospect. You have what the client needs. All the client needs to say is yes to your question, Can we get started next week?

Asking the prospect to buy is a difficult step for many accountants, but it is a vital part of the process. Even though you may feel uncomfortable asking for the business, if you don't, you simply will not get as much new business as you deserve. And who suffers? Both you and the client. You fail to get the client, and the client doesn't get the right services—yours.

6. **Following up** with the client may be as important as identifying new prospects. Follow-up is vital if you are to develop a relationship rather than a one-time sale. All too often, we fail to continue to build the relationship once the sale is made. All buyers go through some type of post-purchase behavior or buyer's remorse. The more expensive and complex the purchase, the more buyers may question whether or not they made the best decision. It is important for you, the seller, to keep in contact with buyers to let them know they did make the right decision and that you are there to continue to meet their needs. At the end of this chapter (see Appendix 2–1), we have included a brief client satisfaction survey that you may want to use with your clients.

As you can see, both buying and selling are complex processes that require time and information. Your goal in consultative sales is to understand how the two processes interact and what your role should be at each step to assist the client in making the best decision.

CLIENTS BUY BENEFITS

Why do clients buy yours or anyone's products and services? Clients make purchases for one reason: to satisfy their needs. In fact, one of the most meaningful definitions of a product or service is a "bundle of benefits." This is one of the simplest concepts in business and sales and one of the most powerful. Yet, most people in sales ignore the benefits the client wants to buy and focus on the features, the details of the products and services they have to sell. So that you never fall into this trap, let's define the two terms.

A **feature** is a characteristic of your product and service. If you were selling a tangible product, you would describe its size, weight, type of construction, and so on. You more than anyone else have in-depth product knowledge. However, just because you can talk about your service features doesn't mean that your prospect or client will be sold. For example, a typical CPA firm describing its capabilities might make the following feature statements:

1. Staff are CPAs with MST degrees. We have 15 years of estate-planning experience.
2. Fully automated tax processing system.
3. Member of National Home Builders Association.
4. Office operates in a Windows environment, and each accountant has a laptop PC.
5. Two offices in the metropolitan area.

Benefits are the values of a feature to the client. In other words, how does a feature help the prospect or client satisfy their needs? The benefit of your service or product answers the question, What is the client really buying? Many times, there are several benefits associated with a feature. For example, the following could be benefits of having a high percentage of senior managers and consultants on your staff:

1. Offers time-tested and innovative planning ideas; less training on your part.
2. Provides access to a network of other professionals.
3. Provides one point of client contact.

Some of the benefits of having an automated in-house tax processing system are as follows:

1. Accelerates refunds; gets tax returns done on time without extensions.
2. In case there is a change in your business or personal status, you'll be able to have a tax projection done at any time throughout the year.

Before you continue, we'd like you to take a few minutes to complete Exercise 2–1.

EXERCISE 2–1
Client Analysis Exercise

List the major reasons that **you** would give a client to buy from your firm. Don't worry if you can't come up with 10 of them. Some of the reasons may be tangible; place a "T" after those items. Others may be intangible; put an "I" after those items. Some of the reasons may be exclusive to your firm; place an "E" after those items.

1. _____ ( )
2. _____ ( )
3. _____ ( )
4. _____ ( )
5. _____ ( )
6. _____ ( )
7. _____ ( )
8. _____ ( )
9. _____ ( )
10. _____ ( )

Now, we want you to do Exercise 2–2. This one is just the opposite of the first one.

EXERCISE 2–2

List the reasons a **client** would give for having bought a service from your firm. Again place a "T" after the items that are tangible, an "I" after those that are intangible, and an "E" after those that are exclusive to your firm.

1. _____ ( )
2. _____ ( )
3. _____ ( )
4. _____ ( )
5. _____ ( )
6. _____ ( )
7. _____ ( )
8. _____ ( )
9. _____ ( )
10. _____ ( )

How did the two lists match up? Unfortunately, if you are like most accountants, Exercise 2–1 probably listed a lot of features. What this means is that you are still presenting your prospects with features rather than benefits. The answers in Exercise 2–2 should have been much different. For example, say in Exercise 2–1 you listed the following feature: Fifteen years of merger and acquisition experience. In Exercise 2–2, the client response should have been something like this: Provides me with outstanding tax strategies or helps me identify troubled companies to buy at a discount.

Understanding Why Accounting Services are Purchased

If you understand the idea that customers buy benefits not features, you have a large part of the basic knowledge underlying sales. There is one further concept, however, that you need to understand if you really are to be able to form and manage a partnership with a client. That concept is that benefits are linked to a deeper level or reason to buy: **needs**. Needs drive the specific benefits sought by a buyer, which you satisfy with your product/service features. To talk about needs, we must examine both business and personal needs. In many cases, especially with the small business owner, the business needs and the personal needs are intertwined. Furthermore, you must always remember that you must, absolutely must, view needs through the eyes of the prospect or client.

There are certain key words that prospects and clients use when they are expressing a need. The astute accountant will quickly pick up these words and begin to employ the *CPA* method. Whenever a prospect or client says something like the following, you can be sure they are expressing a need:

"I wish I could figure out how to..."
"What we need now is..."
"For the last six months, I have been looking for..."
"I want to improve my cash flow, but I don't know how."

Business Needs

When we think of satisfying needs, we probably think first of business needs: audited financial statements, business plans, financing, strategic planning, profit improvement studies, systems reviews, and so on. These are all important, but even in the largest publicly held corporation, there is some personal need behind the business need. And when you are working with the owner-manager, that personal need often cannot be separated from the business need.

Personal Needs

You must always be aware that you are dealing with people whose view of their corporate needs is based on their personal needs. These needs have a basis in both the individual's basic psychological makeup and in their professional status as members of the organization. Even though they are buying something for the organization, as an individual they have a personal stake in the purchase and its outcome. We have all heard someone say, for example, that he had his ego involved in selecting a prestigious firm to audit the company. Such a statement reveals that the buyer is satisfying a personal need. Perhaps it is the need to be associated with the prestigious firm he feels appropriate for his desired status as an executive as well as simply getting a competent audit. It is simply impossible to make a business decision without one's personal needs coming into play. Only computer-based ordering systems can make such decisions, and we obviously aren't dealing with computers!

Personal needs are probably best explained by the list developed by psychologist Abraham Maslow. We have augmented Maslow's list (see Figure 2–3) to better explain the personal needs reflected in the purchase of accounting products and services. Also note that Maslow contended that individuals seek to satisfy needs based on a hierarchy. That means, in general, that you would seek to satisfy very basic needs such as the need for food and shelter before you would seek to satisfy status needs.

Maslow contended that the basic needs for **survival** were food, shelter, and sex. For today's business decision maker, survival is often the name of the game as the pressures of competition and downsizing become universal. Many decisions will, in fact, be driven by the need to get the lowest price that can make the difference between profit and loss. Other decisions may be driven by the need to not make a costly mistake that may have severe professional or job consequences.

FIGURE 2–3
Maslow's Hierarchy of Needs for Buyers of Accounting Services

---

Self-Actualization & Self-Fulfillment
Knowledge, Self-Respect, Fun & Enjoyment

Leadership
Being Well Respected
Being Perceived by Others as a Leader

Social/Sense of Belonging
Everyone Else Is
Maintaining Relationships with Others

Survival and Security
Food & Shelter
Financial and Professional Security

The desire to be a **member of the group** (social sense of belong-ing) is indeed a basic human need. Major publicly held corporations and those companies that are making an initial public offering (IPO) usually want a member of the "Big Six" or other national accounting firms to audit their statements. There is a certain satisfaction knowing that one of these firms is your auditor. If you are not part of the Big Six or other national accounting firm, you probably won't get this type of engagement. The decision maker will feel a need to select one of the best known firms. This way, if something goes wrong he or she can always say: "I don't know what happened. I picked the best firm out there. It wasn't my fault, it was their fault." Imagine if that deci-sion maker had selected a small local accounting firm. The dialogue would have been: "Why did you pick this firm that no one had ever heard of? It was a very poor decision on your part."

There is no denying that **status** also can play a part in many of the decisions we make as individuals and just as surely in our decisions in business. You don't have to be one of the largest firms in the market to have status or be seen by others as a leader in your community. If your clients are saying to others in the marketplace "Do you know what my accountant did for me last week?" there is a good chance you have al-ready achieved status.

Clients can satisfy the need for being well respected and being seen by others as **leaders** in their industry if you can make them profitable. Just think for a minute of the most profitable CPA firm in your area or the most profitable bank, retailer, restaurant, and so on. Aren't they all looked upon as leaders? All offer a superior service or product

A the top of Maslow's pyramid of need is **self-actualization.** Clients who feel they are successful and have reached their level of accomplishment will have a completely different set of needs to fulfill. You may be servicing a wealthy individual who is more interested in leaving a large sum to a university or charity. His or her business becomes secondary to these other needs of accomplishment and self-fulfillment.

The Secret: Learn How to Link Needs, Features, and Benefits

So there it is: Clients are buying benefits to satisfy their needs. As you learned in Exercise 2–1, you may be trying to sell features, but you really need to be able to link the ability of the benefits of your products and services to satisfying client needs. Let's look at an example of how this can be done. One of the greatest needs most business are experiencing today that may be satisfied by accounting firms is in the area of profit improvement. There isn't a business out there today that doesn't need to become more profitable. They may want to achieve this through many different methods, increasing sales, decreasing overhead, creating new products or services, expanding into new markets, acquiring competitors, and so on.

We have found that our consulting clients gain tremendous insight into their business, marketing, and sales activities by simply evaluating what they offer and what clients buy in terms of benefits, and features. Exercise 2–3 requires you to identify features, benefits, and needs. Identify a key product or service your firm offers and list the features you talk about most when selling the product or service or that appears in your promotional literature. Next make a list of all the benefits that a prospect or client could receive from the product or services you offer. When you have the second list completed, you will have the key benefit points you will want to discuss with existing clients and prospects. When you talk in terms of benefits, not only will more people listen to you, more people buy from you.

EXERCISE 2–3
Customer Needs versus Product Features

Service/Product _____

FEATURE	*BENEFIT*	*NEED*

Now, try to think like a client and think about the needs that this service or product may satisfy. We've put benefits in the middle column because this is where you, the seller, and the buyer must come together. The buyer is really buying benefits to satisfy needs, and you are really selling benefits to satisfy those needs. After our consulting clients have gone though several such exercises, they have thrown away a year's supply of brochures that were full of their product/service features but said nothing about satisfying client needs and benefits. Make sure your brochures and verbal communications are filled with benefits, not features.

NOT ALL BUYING DECISIONS ARE THE SAME

To totally understand how a potential client actually satisfies his or her needs, you must understand a little more about different types of buying decisions and how different individuals within the client firm take on different roles as the decision is made. Some types of decisions are necessarily more difficult and complex for a potential client to make and hence will require a different strategy. Few decisions today are made by a single individual. You need to know who in a firm has what influence in the decision to purchase your services. Even when you think that there is only one decision maker, there may be a spouse, child, or other advisor who could have a significant impact on the buyer's decision.

Which Type of Buying Decision Are You Dealing With?

Every buy decision can be categorized into one of the three following types: straight rebuy, modified rebuy, and new buy. It's important to know what type of buy situation you are dealing in. The three types of buying decisions differ in the amount of risk for the buyer and the amount of information the buyer needs to make a purchase decision.

1. **The straight rebuy** presents the least amount of risk to the buyer. If it is just a repeat purchase, in other words, deciding to use your firm again for next year's audit, there will be very little risk to the client. This type of buy is the fulfillment of a recurring need on a regular basis, and generally the buyer selects the same product or service as the last time if that product or service was satisfactory. There are, however, situations where the buyer is in a straight rebuy situation but decides to replace the current supplier. For the most part, the client knows what he or she wants but decides to look at alternatives. This could be due to fees, chemistry, service quality, or competitive pressure.

2. **The modified rebuy** occurs when something in the client's situation has changed or the product/service changes slightly. Because there are new variables in the equation, the buyer will feel a higher degree of risk and will seek additional information before making a purchase decision. To counter this, you will usually need to spend more time educating the client on your services and thier benefits, and further developing the personal relationship. The modified rebuy often requires that a new member of your firm become part of the service team. In addition, this type of situation also includes other influencers, users, gatekeepers, and decision makers from the client's organization. (Don't worry; we will tell you more about the roles these members of the buying firm play in decision making in the next section.)

3. **The new buy** is the most complex decision. Here the client is purchasing a service or product for the very first time. In such situations, firms are frequently sending out requests for proposals (RFPs) to come up with a short list of possible vendors and to learn more about what is available in the marketplace. The buyer will often get many others in the firm involved in the buying process since there is a high degree of risk for the buyer. This type of situation often involves many competitors. If you want to be more successful, your sales

presentations skills will have to be top-notch. And since the client is at risk, you will want to document as much as possible the verifiable benefits of your services; for example, testimonial letters from existing clients for whom you provided a similar service, articles that you may have written on the topic, and even bringing the client on site to another firm where you have performed the same or similar engagement.

Make Sure You Know Who Makes the Decision

The inclusion of more than one person makes the buying decision more complex then we often think. Basically, the buying decision includes anyone inside and sometimes outside of the organization who may play one or more of the following roles. A large purchase decision and one with greater risk to the individual or the firm will usually involve several of the following players.

1. **Users.** For most of the readers of this book, the end user is the business owner, chief financial officer, or controller But as we saw above, depending upon the buying situation, several other people can get involved in the buying decision. The user then is anyone within the organization who will ultimately use the product or service you are providing. If you are selling an accounting system, the actual user could be the firm's bookkeeper, not the owner.

2. **Influencers.** Anyone, whether inside or outside the organization, who directly or indirectly has an impact on the decision-making process should be considered an influencer in the process. Receptionists and secretaries can be influencers as well as members of the board of directors and everyone in between. We have seen some firms lose a bid merely because the accountants were not friendly to the president's secretary.

3. **Buyers.** Many times, the buyer and the user are one and the same person. We define the buyer as the individual or individuals within the organization who have the actual contact with suppliers and arrange the contractual details of the purchase. The buyer is often charged with determining the terms and scope of the purchase. In small companies, it will often be the owner who is the buyer, but as we saw above, the user may be someone else. Here's another example: The owner purchases new computers for his administrative personnel. The users obviously are the secretaries, office manager, and so on.

4. **Deciders.** These are the people within and outside the organization who have the power to approve the final vendor. Many times, buyers and deciders are the same people, especially in a straight rebuy situation and in smaller organizations.
5. **Gatekeepers.** Of all the people involved in the buying process, these may be the most important. Although they usually don't have official veto power, as the name implies, these are people within the organization who can keep you out or let you in. They can do this by controlling the flow of information to the users, influencers, buyers, and deciders. In some cases, a gatekeeper will keep you from ever talking with the real decision makers. Make sure you know who the gatekeepers are and learn how to work with these people.

Appendix 2–1
SAMPLE CLIENT SATISFACTION SURVEY

If you are going to use a client satisfaction survey, these are the types of questions you should be asking your clients:

Directions:

For each of the following questions, your clients should circle one number form 1 to 10, 1 being a negative answer and 7 being very positive.

Note: This question should be laid out:

Directions:

	Never	Sometimes	Always
	1 2	3 4 5	6 7
1. Do you feel that our services provide you with exceptional value?	1 2	3 4 5	6 7
2. If you had a business problem, would you think of calling us first?	1 2	3 4 5	6 7
3. Do you feel we try to gain an understanding of your business problems?	1 2	3 4 5	6 7
4. Do we explain to you the benefits of our services?	1 2	3 4 5	6 7
5. Do you feel the value you receive is in line with the fees we charge?	1 2	3 4 5	6 7
6. Would you recommend us to another business?	1 2	3 4 5	6 7
7. Would you use us again for this service?	1 2	3 4 5	6 7
8. Did we provide our services as promised and in a timely fashion?	1 2	3 4 5	6 7
9. Did we provide you with personal and courteous attention?	1 2	3 4 5	6 7
10. Is there anyone on our service team that you would like to give specia recognition to?	1 2	3 4 5	6 7

Turning Leads into Prospects

"Leads are all around us; we just don't see them."

August Aquila

INTRODUCTION

The accountants we consult with often ask us, "Where do I find leads so I can start to sell?" Leads and prospects are all around us; we just don't see them. In fact, everyone you meet is either a prospective client or knows someone who is. However, prospecting takes time and talent. It's similar to panning for gold. You need to know where to look and how to do it. This chapter will lead you through the process of turning leads into prospects. The first thing you need to accept about developing prospects is that it doesn't happen by accident. There is a learnable process to lead generation and prospecting. We will show you how to identify target prospects, methods to develop leads, how to qualify leads so you don't waste a lot of time chasing down blind alleys, and ways to follow up with the leads you generate.

SELF-ASSESSMENT 3–1: NETWORKING

To help you determine how good you are at developing leads, we have included the following networking self-assessment. Take a few minutes and circle the appropriate answer.

1. How many business associates, clients, other professionals, and so on do you see or talk to on a regular basis throughout the year?

   a. 5–10   b 10–20   c. More than 20

2. How many contacts do you have that have been a good source of referrals?

    a. 1–3   b. 3–7   c. More than 7

3. Do you make it a practice to directly ask for leads or referrals when appropriate?

    a. Never   b. Sometimes   c. Often

4. Do you systematically maintain communication with your network on a regular basis?

    a. Rarely   b. When I think about it c. Regular and often

5. Do you promptly follow up on promises or commitments you have made?

    a. Rarely   b. Sometimes   c. Always

6. Do you work out referral exchanges with other professionals?

    a. Rarely   b. Sometimes   c. Often

7. Do you actively seek to do favors for network members?

    a. Rarely   b. Sometimes   c. Often

8. Do you make a special acknowledgement of referrals sent your way?

    a. Rarely   b. Sometimes   c. Always

9. Have you met the professionals that your clients depend on (bankers, lawyers, personal financial planners, consultants, etc.)?

    a. Very few   b. Some   c. Most of them

10. Do you initially consider new acquaintances as a potential source of new business referrals?

    a. Never   b. Sometimes   c. Usually

11. Do you view social gatherings as an opportunity to meet new business contacts as well as to socialize?

    a. No   b. Sometimes   c. Often

12. Do you like to meet new people?

    a. No   c. Yes

Add up your total points. Each a = 1 point, b = 2 points, and c = 3 points (maximum 36).

Total Score:

32–36: You are doing a great job! Share your skills with others.

22–32: With more focused attention, your network could be "hot"!

12–22: Time to get your head out of those books!

(Source: Reprinted with permission checkers Simon & Rosner, CPAs, Chicago Il.)

LEAD AND PROSPECT
IDENTIFICATION PROCESS

Step 1: Identifing Target Prospects

The process begins (see Figure 3–1) by determining the profile of your target prospects, the group of businesses or individuals you believe most likely to be clients for your services. There are over 11 million identifiable firms in the United States and perhaps tens of millions of individuals who might make use of services such as estate and tax planning or basic tax return preparation. If you don't narrow down your targets, you may end up actually doing nothing because you'll have too many leads to chase. Or you'll find that you are wasting your valuable time and money pursuing leads that don't fit your firm or are unlikely to become clients. You need to develop a target profile of those firms or individuals worth the time and money you will invest in the selling effort.

The best way to find more clients like the ones you have is to look at your current client base and analyze your business and individual clients. Take a few minutes now and jot down on a sheet of paper answers to the following questions about your clients (see Exercise 3–1). Once you have identified the type of prospect you are looking for, isolate the individuals, businesses, or associations that are associated with those prospects. For example, if your targets are physicians and you know that physician office managers belong to the Medical Group Management Association, you need to become active in the local chapter of that association. That's where you will find leads for this target. If your targets are contractors, you will need to get involved in the various construction associations and develop relationships with the bonding companies in your area because that is where these leads will be.

FIGURE 3–1
Lead and Prospect Identification Process

```
                                    | Step 4: Turning Leads into Prospects
                          | Step 3: Qualifying Leads
                | Step 2: Finding Leads
      | Step 1: Identifying Target Prospects
```

EXERCISE 3–1:

Businesses:

1. **What industries do my clients represent?** It's quite surprising that when we ask accountants to segment their existing clients into industries, the typical answers that come back are, "I don't have any special industries that I serve" or, "I didn't know that 30 percent of my clients were in that one industry." It's surprising how little accountants know about their existing clients. If you have assigned SIC (Standard Industrial Classification) codes to your clients and this information is on your time and billing system or database, this exercise will be very easy to complete. If you don't have SIC codes assigned to your clients, take your 20 to 25 highest billing clients and determine what industries they are in. Sooner or later, you will need to be able to identify target prospects by their SIC codes. The SIC is far more than the code some use for filing with the IRS. Identifying target prospects by SIC will allow you to literally find the location, address, phone number, and key contact person of every firm in the nation with that SIC.

2. **Geographic location?** If you are looking for new clients, it is often a good idea to determine where your existing clients are located because they usually know other business owners or individuals who live or work near them. For most CPA firms, location is not a primary factor in describing their ideal client. What is important is knowing whether or not the target company is headquarters or just a branch office. If the company is just a branch, the chance of obtaining accounting work is slim.

3. **Size (volume, number of employees)?** Being able to define your clients by their sales volume and number of employees is frequently an excellent way to further identify your client base. For example, if you know that your ideal client is a manufacturer with a sales volume between $3 million and $5 million, fewer than 50 employees, and is headquartered in your area, you can purchase a list of those firms that fit this description.

Individuals

In the same manner that you analyzed your business clients, you need to examine the types of individual clients you are currently servicing in order to seek more. What do you really know about your clients?

1. **Net worth?** If you are building an individual tax and consulting practice, you will want to be able to segment your clients by their net worth. Individual clients who have a high net worth are excellent leads for estate planning and other types of tax planning and investment-type consulting.
2. **Geographic location?** Is there any pattern to where your individual clients live? Do they belong to the same country club, church, or synagogue? Try to find patterns among your clients.
3. **Income level?** This information is readily available through their tax returns. You might be surprised to find out that 20 percent of your tax return clients could produce 60–80 percent of your tax preparation and consulting revenues.
4. **Occupation?** Make sure you segment your clients by occupation. You may be surprised to find out that 15 percent of your individual clients are engineers or golf pros, for example. These may be new niches for your to develop.

If you still haven't done it, take a few minutes now and jot down on a sheet of paper your description of your ideal business and individual client.

Step 2: Finding Leads

Now that you have identified your target prospects, the next step is to find them. There are two sources of leads: **direct leads** through people you know and **indirect leads** through secondary sources. You should first generate direct leads from people you know socially or professionally. These leads are more valuable, and you are more likely to turn them into new clients. You may even be able to go beyond getting a cold lead to obtaining a referral. Since you will eventually exhaust your existing friends and acquaintances for leads, you must constantly seek to expand your network of acquaintances. Second, you can obtain indirect leads systematically from your direct marketing program, from research, and from lists you carefully match to your target profile. We will begin with direct leads.

Direct Leads. "Leads are all around us; we just don't see them." When we make this statement to many accountants, they just roll their eyes and say "If there are so many leads out there, how come I can't find any of them?" Once you become sales oriented, you start doing things differently to find the leads to meet your lead goals. You will become aware of the leads around you when you become observant and start to take some risks. Here are some real-life situations where leads have been developed because the individual took advantage of the situation.

On a trip from Chicago to the West Coast, a consultant we know was fortunate to be sitting catty-corner from a law firm administrator who started talking about the law firm and various pension and benefits issues that had come up over the past few months. Although it was an area in which the consultant had little experience, he knew that he had partners in the firm who could address the issues at hand. All he really needed to do was to ask if the administrator would be interested in talking to his partner. She said yes, and a lead was developed. (By the way, it turned into a $35,000 engagement.)

A CPA we know was waiting in an airport on a Sunday afternoon. He soon found himself sitting next to another gentleman with a suit. The usual conversation began, and before long the accountant had developed a lead to do some consulting for the gentleman who turned out to be a physician.

Many CPA firms today provide their staff with lapel pins with the firm logo. A partner in a firm in a major city told us that he was stopped in an elevator and asked what the pin meant. When he said he was with a CPA and consulting firm, the gentleman told him he was looking for a new accountant and wondered if he would be interested in proposing on their audit.

What do these three situations have in common? None of them was part of a planned marketing program activity nor did the lead come from traditional lead sources. In each case, the three professionals saw or did something that most other accountants wouldn't. They *did not* let the opportunity go by. They took a risk, albeit a small one, and started talking to a stranger. Their risks paid off. Think of circumstances in which you were involved that could have lead to new business opportunities. Making a major purchase—furniture or a car, for example—or even a small purchase provides you with an excellent opportunity to talk with a business owner. All you really need to do is to talk with people. (Chapters 5 and 6) will help you develop the skills you need to feel comfortable in doing this.)

The Best Lead Comes from a Referral.   We carefully differentiate between a lead and a referral. A lead is only the identity of someone or some firm that might potentially be a prospect. A referral is a personal recommendation from a current client or referral source that is, in effect, an introduction to a target prospect. Even if the person making the referral doesn't personally make the contact, he or she is expressing the belief that you can satisfy the needs of the firm or person referred. The person making the referral has a personal stake and is vouching for you and your firm's ability. Referrals can be professional or personal. Professional referrals will come from satisfied customers. But friends and acquaintances who infer you will provide quality accounting services based on a nonaccounting social relationship are also good sources of references. Remember, you are always making a personal and professional impression that could turn into business. Many professionals forget this. An action today can have a positive or negative impact on your practice tomorrow. People will often judge your professional skills and quality on nonbusiness or professional activities. Selling and marketing are like planting seeds. You need to nurture the seed so that it produces fruit. It doesn't happen overnight.

Cultivating a Network for Direct Leads.   To develop direct leads, you need to use your existing network of acquaintances and aggressively establish opportunities to meet new people to find new leads. Figure 3–2 lists some basic ideas on how to meet people. (Figure 3–3 indicates what not to do if you really want to meet people.) In her book *Mega Networking,* Melissa Giovagnoli provides 101 ways to help you develop your networking skills. Readers who want to further enhance their skills in this areas should read Giovagnoli's book.

David Dworski, in his article "Social Selling" (*Sales and Marketing,* December 1990, p. 46) explains the seven deadly sins of socializing. Just as it is necessary to know what to do, it is also necessary to know what not to do. When networking, remember these deadly mistakes.

Finally, we have enclosed an example of a follow up letter (see Appendix 3–1) from a personal "network" meeting. The letter assumes that during the time spent with the individual you talked about a potential need.

Now it is time for you to do some more work (see Exercise 3–2). These exercises are an important part of this book. So don't skip over them. You will find that doing each exercise will help you become more efficient at selling your services. They will also help you to remember the four we posed in the Introduction.

1. How can I put what I am reading to use right now?

2. How should I change my current way of doing business development to become more efficient?
3. How should I be changing my current way of thinking about selling my firm's professional services?
4. How will what I am reading help me to better service my clients?

FIGURE 3–2
How to Meet People

There are countless ways to meet people in order to start the prospecting cycle. The following are the most typical suggestions we hear from successful accountants who sell:
• Say hello! Be friendly.
• Have a goal to meet one new person per week.
• Network.
• Become a famous person. A famous person is someone who has several clients in the industry, speaks at industry association meetings, writes articles for the profession, and is considered an expert in the field.
• Become active in a trade or professional association.

FIGURE 3–3
How Not to Meet People
The Seven Deadly Sins

1. Failing to set a goal
2. Using someone you know as a social "crutch" for the event and staying with them
3. Hiding in a corner/sitting down early
4. Failing to introduce yourself
5. Being inattentive to whomever you are talking with
6. Staying too long
7. Failing to follow up

EXERCISE 3–2:
Current Lead Sources

For each of the categories listed below, identify a specific individual or two who are either lead sources or referral sources. This is the beginning of your referral network. It is important to keep these people apprised of your activities, successes, and the fact that you are always looking for new clients. It's also critical that you feed your sources with either referrals or other information so that they remain healthy and strong. As we have said in this chapter, leads are all around you; you just need to look for them.

	Lead Sources	Referral Sources
1. Family		
2. Close friends		
3. Bankers		
4. Attorneys		
5. Insurance agents		
6. Stock brokers		
7. Trade and professional associations		
8. Seminars you attend		
9. Businesspeople		
10. Church/synagogue		
11. Doctors		
12. Neighbors		
13. Spouse's employer		
14. Kids' parents		

If you can't complete this exercise, you have gaps in your lead sources. Start to fill those gaps now!

How to Ask for a Lead or Referral.   There is a simple process to follow in knowing how to ask for leads. If you follow one of the methods we have laid out below, you can dramatically increase your lead generation success.

Now that you have identified your ideal targets, it's time to *schedule a meeting* to ask for a lead or referral. There are basically two ways to ask for leads (reciprocal and nonreciprocal methods). No matter which approach you take, it is always necessary to ask in a positive fashion. You never want to imply to a referral source or client that you are desperately looking for new business.

The best way to put into practice what you are now reading is to do the following: Determine how you will ask for a lead or referral and *practice out loud*. If you are going to be asking another professional for a lead, you should consider using what is known as the *reciprocal method*. In other words, you are exchanging leads with this referral source.

Example: You are speaking to a lending officer at a local bank. "It seems we have a similar client base. Often we're in the position of referring our clients to major banks. Do you refer your clients to accounting firms? Which ones? Why don't we work out an arrangement to help each other out?"

The *nonreciprocal* approach is appropriate when you ask a satisfied client, friend, or other professional for leads. There are different ways to accomplish this.

There is nothing wrong with making a specific request.

Example: "We've developed a strong reputation in employee benefits consulting. Would you introduce me to Joe Smith at XYZ Corp? I think we can help him."

or

"Mary, I've been trying to meet the new owner at the auto dealership in town. Do you think you could arrange a lunch for the three of us?"

There are times when you may want to be a little less direct and make more of general request from a satisfied client or other professional.

Example: "Thanks for the compliment, Joe. We've had a lot of experience in the employee benefits area. Is there anyone else you think we should meet? We're always looking for new clients."

Finally, there are opportunities to ask for a referral when a satisfied client or other professional truly understands a specific service of yours.

Example: You just finished providing computer training for the internal accounting staff of a manufacturing client. The request might go as follows: "Can you think of anyone who needs this kind of training? Would you mind calling them and letting them know I'll be in touch? Thanks."

Before we end our discussion on direct leads, we want to share with you some helpful strategies we have learned. These are simple constructs you need to remember to generate direct leads.

1. **Always keep business cards with you.** We can't tell you how many times we've met accountants who did not have any business cards with them. How do you respond to someone who asks for your business card when you don't have one? Always keep 5–10 cards in your wallet or purse.

2. **Ask your referral sources to have lunch with you occasionally.** There is a lot of truth in the expression "out of sight, out of mind." Remember, these referral sources are giving

business to someone. If it's not you, you probably aren't spending enough time with them. Don't be shy about asking your referral sources the following question: "It's been a long time since you've given me any referrals; is there something I need to do differently?" Or you might want to say, "Mary, I'm interested in expanding my practice and would certainly appreciate any future referrals you could give me."

3. If one of your sources is promoted or changes jobs, be sure to **send a congratulatory letter.** Everyone likes to be recognized for their accomplishments. You will definitely score some points with your referral sources by acknowledging their professional successes.

4. **Find out what associations your referral sources belong to** and what positions they hold. If these are niche associations you want to target, it is probably a good idea to join the association and become active in it. Try joining the membership committee or the program committee. Both of these will get you more leads than you will be able to handle. The membership committee gives you an excellent reason to contact leads on behalf of the association. It's a great way to meet others in a nonthreatening way. Being on the program committee will allow you to get a friend or associate on one of the programs. Either way, you will score additional points.

5. **Get to be known as a doer** and get to know the important people in your community and your niches. Once you are known as a contributor and a doer, your prospects and referral sources will make judgements about your professional skills based on the way you work with the association.

Appendix 3–2 provides a sample prospecting letter to a lead that you received from a referral source.

Indirect Leads.   Indirect leads and techniques to acquire them have many advantages over direct leads as well as many disadvantages. Like direct leads, indirect leads require that you have a good profile of your targets. Leads from indirect sources are often called "cold" leads because you generally do not know if the firm or individual you have identified has recognized that a problem exists and that they have a need.

During the last several years, many accounting firms have begun to use direct mail techniques, advertising, and even telemarketing to develop indirect leads. The main resources for indirect leads are trade and professional association directories and mailing lists that can be purchased from companies such as Dun & Bradstreet, Contacts Influential, and various list brokers. Lists brokers will often provide you with customized lists. For example, you could request a list of high net worth individuals by zip codes. These would definitely be leads for your tax or estate planning services.

When you use mailing lists and list brokers as lead sources, the issue is not how many leads and names you can find but how to identify the true prospects. Most mailing list companies provide basic information about the company's name, address, phone number, and contact person. They usually sort the companies by SIC codes, sales volume, and number of employees. SIC codes can sometimes be misleading since many firms have a primary and secondary SIC code. Make sure you know what you are asking for when buying a list. You need to work closely with the list broker supplying your lists if you are to minimize the number of worthless names and maximize the number of true prospects you attempt to qualify.

Using Direct Marketing Efforts to Find Leads. Because most direct-marketing efforts generate many leads and few prospects, we recommend that you begin the indirect lead-finding process with a letter. You should include a response card whenever you use direct mail to develop leads. In fact, a letter and response card combination is probably the best way to reach all leads initially. Not only is a letter relatively inexpensive, it provides an excellent means for you to begin to establish your firm's credibility and position.

If you are going to use the indirect approach, you will want to find a direct-mail specialist to help you put together a winning campaign. Here are some basic questions you should ask yourself about every direct mail piece that leaves your office:

1. Does the mailing piece look like junk mail? If it does, it is not the right piece for your firm to be sending out.
2. Have you defined in your mind and is it clearly stated in the letter what you want the reader to do when he or she receives the mailing piece?
3. How easy is it for the reader to respond? Did you enclose a business reply card?
4. Is the copy easy to read? Is your message complicated or simple?

5. Why should the reader believe what you have to say? Do you have any testimonials? What types of guarantees are you offering?

6. Direct mail is not a one-time effort. The key to developing leads through this method is repetition. Do you have a real direct-mail campaign, or are you doing a one-time mailing?

Appendix 3–3 provides you with a sample prospecting letter from a cold-lead list. There are several excellent marketing books that will give you a better understanding of direct marketing techniques. Two that you should consult are *The Marketing Advantage,* published by the AICPA MAP Committee (New York: AICPA, 1994) and *Competing for Clients in the 90s,* written by Bruce Marcus (Chicago: Probus, 1992).

Finally, before we move on to qualifying leads, we want to tell you two more things about leads.

1. There are leads you can follow up with personally. In other words, you can take the lead all the way to the close by yourself. Depending upon your firm and your position in it, the leads you should actively pursue are usually those you can personally act on.

2. There are leads you should refer to someone else in your firm. These are often the leads that are beyond your areas of expertise or would be better served by another individual within your firm. One survey respondent had this to say: "The most successful accountants are the ones who realize what they can and cannot do for a prospect or client." Don't be afraid to share your leads with others in the firm. If the firm doesn't close a new client, no one wins.

Step 3: Qualifying Leads

Qualifying leads will vary depending on whether you are generating direct leads or indirect leads. Because you can generate so many leads, although many may be quite cold, the qualifying process is vital if you are to use your time effectively. Qualifying takes time and effort. You don't necessarily want every lead as a client. Before you invest time and effort on a lead, take them through a qualification process. For most accounting firms, this is a three-step process. Each firm needs to determine its own criteria for qualifying leads, but generally you will want to determine the following:

1. The need the prospect wants to satisfy.
2. The ability of the prospect to buy the service.
3. What the prospect can or will pay.

First, determine what services your prospect needs. Are they services your firm offers? Are they services your firm wishes to emphasize? What kind of realization can the firm expect on this work? With price cutting prevalent in audit work these days, a new audit client may not be nearly as attractive as a client in need of more profitable consulting work. On the other hand, a large new audit client often means an opportunity to cross-sell a broad range of add-on services. Compare the costs and benefits of getting each potential client to the revenues they will generate and the time your firm must invest.

Second, determine the prospect's ability and authority to buy. There are two concerns here. One, is your contact at the prospect company a decision maker? If not, he or she may desire your services but has no authority to buy them. You could waste a lot of time on someone who can't make a decision. Two, is the company itself a good prospect for the service? A small retailer might ask you about upgrading its point-of-sale system when its current system is more than adequate for its needs. In both cases, you shouldn't give up but should redirect your efforts. If you aren't dealing with a decision maker, get your contact to introduce you to someone with purchasing authority. If the prospect company doesn't need or isn't ready for your services, by all means tell them so. Selling an unneeded service could mean an unhappy client. Giving good advice could mean another engagement in a different area or at least that they'll call you when they do need the service. That's what the consultative approach is all about.

Third, determine what the prospect will or can pay. No matter how desperately a prospect needs your services, no matter how ready they may be to buy, if they can't afford to pay the bill, you must seriously reevaluate going after their business. If they can pay, but don't recognize the value of your service, examine what competitors are charging for similar services or seek to further demonstrate the value of your service to the client. In Exercise 3–3, we provide a series of questions you should ask to qualify a lead.

EXERCISE 3–3
Lead-Qualifying Analysis

The following analysis will help you qualify leads. Before moving on in the sales effort, make sure you have answered the following questions.

                                                   Yes   No   ?

1. Does my lead client have a real need?
2. Does the lead recognize his or her need, or can I show them they have a need?
3. Is my lead committed to solving their need?
4. Does the lead fit the industry where I can deliver experience and expertise?
5. Do I have a viable solution to their need?
6. Have sufficient funds been allocated, or are funds available for my solution?
7. If required, can I provide a sound cost justification for any solution?
8. Have I identified the decision maker and key recommender?
9. Can I get to the decision maker?
10. Can I get the agreement of the key recommender?
11. Do I know the decision criteria?
12. Can I get the lead to commit time, resources, and dollars to examine my suggested solution?
13. Do I know my competition?
14. Do I know what the lead likes or dislikes about the existing CPA firm, and can I communicate our strategies effectively?
15. Does research and history indicate that my lead is tied into a CPA firm? Do I have a plan for change?

Step 4: Turning Leads into Prospects

Once you determine that the lead has a need you can satisfy, the ability and authority to buy your product or service, and the dollars to spend, the lead becomes a prospect.

ABC Prospects.   Once you begin the systematic process of prospecting we have outlined above, you will find that you have generated so many prospects that you will need to even further refine your categories of prospects to reflect your evaluation of their potential worth to your firm as clients and how much effort should be spent to turn them into clients. This is usually done with an A, B, and C ranking of prospects, A's being your best prospects and C's your worst. This ranking generally includes the potential fee, potential profitability, and of course your initial estimate of the likelihood of converting a prospect into a client. A, B, and C prospects are different for each firm. Most firms we have consulted with determine their ranking based on the overall fee that the prospect would generate and the likelihood that the prospect will with become a client in the next 60 to 90 days. The important thing is that you put your initial energies toward your A prospects.

Lead and Prospect Goal Setting.   Even though leads and prospects are all around us it is easy to ignore them, just as it is easy to kick a lump of precious stone out of the way as you would any other rock. Not only do you have to be looking for leads if you want to really find them, you need to establish goals for the number of leads and prospects you want to generate. Setting personal goals makes you constantly aware of the need to look for leads and then turn them into prospects.

Goal setting or managing your own behavior is a process we will discuss in Chapter 11. For the time being, we just want to give you some insights into the power of goal setting and how it can work for you. Most people do not have written goals. Studies have shown that those who have taken the time to write down their goals outperform everyone else. For example, if you want to meet four new prospects per month and you think your existing client base can provide you with the necessary leads, you might have to talk to at least five clients per week to eventually reach your goal. Briefly stated, your goal might read as follows: By December 31, 19XX, I will have met four new prospects per month for the months of September, October, November, and December. Writing this goal down, and outlining the necessary action steps will help you achieve it. Just remember this: "As it is written, so shall it happen."

As you can easily see, prospects have a much higher value to you than leads. With the basic information you have at hand, you are now ready to move on to the second step in the selling cycle: setting up an initial appointment. This is the topic of our next chapter.

See p. 52-53.

Appendix 3–1
SAMPLE FOLLOW UP LETTER

Mr. Eugene Hall
123 South Street
Your City, USA

Dear Gene:

It was certainly a pleasure meeting you today at the monthly meeting of the Manufacturers' Roundtable Group. Although this was my first meeting of the year, everyone made me feel quite welcome.

I know we only had a few minutes to discuss some of the issues you are currently facing at your company. I will call you next week. I'm planning to be in the area and would like to get a better understanding of what you are trying to accomplish.

I'm looking forward to seeing you.

Sincerely,

Eagle & Associates
Louis Eagle, CPA

Appendix 3–2
SAMPLE PROSPECTING LETTER FOR LEAD FROM REFERRAL SOURCE

Emily Haliziw
Haliziw & Associates
1632 Street
New City, USA

Dear Ms. Haliziw:

Our mutual friend, Robert Jones, of First National Bank suggested that I contact you. He has informed me that you are currently considering a change of accountants and felt that our services could be of value to you and your company.

I'd like to meet you to determine your needs and how we can best serve them. I'll be calling you next week to set up an appointment. If you would like to call me, my direct number is 555-5555.

Sincerely,

John Friendly, CPA

P.S. I'm enclosing a copy of our firm's capabilities brochure as well as the most recent copy of our bimonthly family business newsletter.

Appendix 3–3
SAMPLE PROSPECTING LETTER FOR INDIRECT LEAD FROM MAILING LIST

Mr. Lloyd Cullum
233 East Street
Poplar City, USA

Dear Mr. Cullum:

Improve your collections and other vital operating areas with a management evaluation survey for your firm. The survey, performed by our Law Firm Services Group, evaluates every area of law firm practice management, yet takes only a couple of hours of your firm administrator's time. We have performed these surveys for more than 15 firms in the area and have included a list of satisfied clients that you may want to call. The cost is just $500—a small investment that can yield tremendous benefits by highlighting opportunities for growth and giving you a detailed diagnosis of your firm's current management practices. If you do not feel our reviews have provided you with value, we will not charge you.

I will call next week to arrange a meeting with you to discuss the benefits your firm can realize from this low-cost, high-value service. Feel free to call me or return the enclosed business reply card.

Sincerely,

Michael D. Allan, CPA

Chapter Four

Planning Your Way to Successful Sales Calls

INTRODUCTION

In the previous chapter, you found out how to identify and qualify leads. Now with your list of prospects in hand, you will want to move to the next step: setting up successful sales calls. If your prospects come from referrals, you'll find this step fairly easy. However, if the majority of your leads are indirect, you, or someone who works for you, will have to be extremely dedicated to setting up appointments. Finally, a new business sales call is as much an art as it is a science. This chapter will teach you how to contact prospects in order to set up the initial meeting and then how to plan for your initial sales call.

SELF ASSESSMENT 4–1: SECURING SALES CALLS

Answer the following statements yes or no. This self-assessment will give you some idea of what you will need to work on in order to secure more successful sales calls.

	Yes	No
1. I have a systematic process that I follow whenever I have a new business opportunity.		
2. I feel comfortable setting up initial sales calls.		
3. I have written reasons why a prospect should see me.		

4. Prior to the initial sales call, I lay
   out my call strategy.
5. I know what I need to about a prospect's
   industry prior to making the call.

GETTING TO DECISION MAKERS AND MAKING APPOINTMENTS— THE EIGHT STEP *CPA* METHOD

Getting through to decision makers can be frustrating. Only 1 out of 10 messages sent to top executives ever actually gets through. And even when you get to talk to the decision maker, you may hear statements such as these:

- I don't need it.
- I'm too busy to see you now.
- Why don't you call back later?
- I'm satisfied with my current accountant.

Effort, time, and money spent to get leads, and referrals may all go for nothing if you can't arrange a meeting with a prospect. If you qualified your prospects as we suggested in Chapter 3, you won't have to do as much in this stage. We have used the following eight-step approach to getting appointments and would like to share it with you. It will provide you with a systematic approach to getting an appointment:

1. Write before you call.
2. Make friends with the secretary.
3. Ask for the order (i.e., get to your reason for calling).
4. Explain why the decision maker should meet with you.
5. Probe and answer objections.
6. Ask for the appointment.
7. Verify the appointment.
8. Keep notes while speaking.

Oh yes, and one more thing before you ever think of picking up the phone. You must know exactly what you are going to say when the secretary and then the prospect answers the phone.

Write before You Call

If your referral source has introduced you, write a brief letter to the prospect. Introduce yourself and very briefly state why you'd like to meet. Then give a date and time when you will call. This way, your call won't come as a surprise. Rule number one: Call when you said you would. When you sent your letter, you made a promise you must now keep. It's a simple way to prove your dependability. If you're lucky, the prospect will be waiting for your call. However, don't expect to get through on the first try. Remember:

- Not every call turns into a lead.
- Your letter lets decision maker know why you are calling.
- Enclose your firm brochure, newsletters, and so on, with your letter.
- Make the follow-up call four to five days after sending letter.
- The best time to call is early in the morning, at lunch time, and after 5 P.M.

Make Friends with the Secretary

When you get through, tell the secretary who you are and why you are calling. Explain that the prospect is expecting your call. If the prospect is not available, ask when would be a convenient time to call back. Don't just leave a message. Doing this surrenders control of the process and leaves the next step to the prospect. Many executives use secretaries to screen their calls. And often the secretary has considerable discretion in deciding who gets some of the boss's time. Don't antagonize the secretary; don't be aloof or impatient. Take a minute to chat. By becoming a person, instead of just another voice on the phone, you increase your chances of getting through to the decision maker. Here are some points to remember:

- If you call early or late, you may the avoid secretary.
- Secretaries are trained to screen calls.
- Be polite, professional—the secretary is a gatekeeper.

- Find out his or her name. (People like to be called by their name.)
- Prepare a sample script.

Here is a sample conversation you might have with the secretary:

You:	Good afternoon, this is Allan Davids. I'm a partner in the firm of Simons and Davids. [If this is a lead from one of your referral sources, you will definitely want to mention the person who referred you.] Is Mr. Jones in?
Secretary:	No, he is out for the day.
You:	Are you his secretary?
Secretary:	Yes.
You:	May I ask your name?
Secretary:	Mary.
You:	Mary, can you tell me when is the best time to reach Mr. Jones?

By mentioning the secretary's name, you'll be less of a stranger the next time you call. Don't be condescending to secretaries. Don't treat them as adversaries. The secretary has an unspoken agenda. She wants to know the following:

- **What your message is.** To get to the decision maker, you often need to explain why you are calling. That is, you may need to "sell" the screener before you can get through to her boss. You might try saying something such as this: "I'm calling today because we are representing a widget company that is for sale, and I wanted to talk with Mr. Jones to find out whether he is interested in learning more about it."
- **Who you are and why she should let you speak to her boss.** When the secretary says, "Mr. Jones is in a meeting," try responding, "Mary, I also have a very tight schedule today, and I would really like to speak to Mr. Jones. I can call back at 2:00 or 4:30. Which would be better?"

Both you and the secretary need to know whether she or he should pass you on to someone else.

Ask for the Order (i.e., Get to Your Reason for Calling)

You finally have the prospect on the phone. After all the work you've done qualifying and researching the prospect, the urge is to prove how much you know. Resist it. You don't have a second to waste at this stage. The main purpose of your call is to set up a face-to-face meeting. Secondarily, it's a chance to test some of the hypotheses you've developed. In the beginning, let the prospect do the talking. After introducing yourself, reestablish your link with your referral source. If an attorney referred you, say, "Bill Jacobs and I have worked together solving the type of succession issue you're facing, and he suggested I give you a call. Could you give me a little background on your situation?" This gives the prospect a chance to agree that he needs your services.

Once you've established that you have something to talk about, try to set up a meeting. For instance, the prospect might say, "Two of our shareholders will be retiring within the next three to five years. We want to ensure a smooth transition of their interests and avoid any unwelcome outside owners." Instead of launching into a drawn out account of the options available, you'd simply say, "There are a number of strategies available to help you meet these goals. And our firm has helped many clients come to grips with these issues. Instead of taking up too much of your time now, why don't we schedule a meeting so we can discuss your situation in detail?" If the client says yes, you're on your way. But be prepared for resistance. In real life, things don't always go this smoothly.

Remember your goal at each stage of the process. Right now, you want to set up a meeting. If the prospect won't agree to that, try to get him to agree to some intermediary step. For instance, ask if you can send some information for him to review and then schedule a follow-up call to answer any questions. At a minimum, try to schedule another call at a later date.

When you are on the phone with the decision maker, you may have no more than 15 seconds to get to the point. If that is the case, don't start the conversation with a description of your firm or anything else. Instead, ask for the order right away. Here is a sample approach:

"Good morning, Mr. Jones. This is John Mann. I sent you a confidential letter last week, and I am calling to determine your interest. Did you receive it?"

No matter what the response is, continue by saying:

"The letter explained that we have been retained by a well-known client to conduct an acquisition search on its behalf. We have identified your company as a potential candidate for further discussion. Would you be interested in discussing the specifics of our engagement?"

Explain Why the Decision Maker Should Meet with You

The next step is actually a continuation of the previous one. At this stage, you should provide reasons why the decision maker should see you. In other words, explain what's in it for him. If his prospect does not feel that it's worth his time, or feels that someone else in the company should speak to you, you probably won't make a sale. Here are two reasons that you could give the prospect in our example:

- "We have assisted 22 firms in the past 12 months in successfully packaging their businesses for sale. Each company sold for 10 percent more than the owner originally thought he could obtain."
- "Our national network places your business in front of 10,000 qualified buyers every month.

Always keep in mind the purpose of your call— to obtain an appointment, not to sell or close anything over the phone.

Probe and Answer Objections

Once the decision maker is engaged in a conversation, probe for additional information. Often, you will also have to answer objections. However, respond to a maximum of two or three objections; beyond that, just thank the individual for his time and go on to the next call. Let's look at some typical objections CPAs will face:

Objection: "I'm not your client. Why do you want to talk to me?"

Response: "We are currently engaged by one of our clients in your industry to find a qualified buyer for that company. Are you interested in expanding your company through an acquisition? Can we get together next week for a meeting?"

Objection: "I've never heard of [your firm's name].

Response: "We are the fourteenth largest CPA firm in the state. We specialize in small-to-medium-sized closely held and family held businesses. We offer assistance in acquisitions and divestiture of businesses, financing, business planning, tax planning, and accountancy. Our clients tell us we're a profit center for them. May I set up a meeting with you for next week?"

Objection: "Send me something" [e.g., more literature].

Response: "A request for literature, Mr. Jones, usually means that you have some questions I haven't answered yet. What questions do you have?" Or, "I'd be happy to send you that; how serious are you about pursuing...?"

The key is to handle the objections in a professional manner. This is a skill that every successful salesperson must develop. (We will cover this in more detail in Chapter 9.) The key to handling objections is not so much to create answers but to put answers in the proper form, as the above examples have shown. Before calling, make a list of possible objections and write out your responses. Objections can fall into one of the following four categories:

- Service objections.
- Personal objections.
- Postponement objections.
- Price objections.

To handle objections, keep in mind the following ideas:

- **Confirm your understanding of the objection.** This is usually done by repeating it or by saying, "Obviously, something I've said makes you feel that way. Could you tell me what it is?"
- **Acknowledge the objection:** "I know you're a busy executive..."
- **Stress a benefit:** "That's why I'm only asking for one-half hour of your time to explain..."
- **Get back to your sales message:** "Can we set up a meeting next week?"

Ask for the Appointment

In closing, you must ask for the order (which, in this case, is a face-to-face interview). Most sales are lost because the salesperson never asks for the order. How do you do it? Once you ask, "Can we set up a meeting next week?" just pause. Don't say another word. The ball is then in the prospect's court. If you don't jump in, the prospect will have to say something (even if it's not yes).

Verify the Appointment

Before ending the conversation, thank the prospect for his time and verify the appointment time, date, and location. For example, "Mr. Jones, we will look forward to meeting with you on Tuesday the 25th at your place. I just want to verify that I have the correct address and suite number. I'm looking forward to seeing you then."

To further cement the appointment, you should send a brief letter to the prospect indicating the time of the meeting and who will be coming with you. If you have any literature that is appropriate to send at this time, by all means send it.

Keep Notes While Speaking

While on the phone with the prospect, it's best to keep notes. No matter how good your memory is, you won't remember everything; when it's time for the appointment in two weeks, you'll be glad to have notes to refresh your memory. It's important to keep an accurate callback file. Each lead should be followed through until the prospect says yes or no. Finally, to track the effectiveness of your program, keep a prospective business report.

PLANNING FOR THE INITIAL SALES CALL

When we consult with accountants, we find out too often that little, if any, preparation is done prior to making the initial face-to-face sales call. Therefore, our first bit of advice is this: Know what you are going to do at the initial sales call. Figure 4–1 provides you with a simplified sales call plan, and Figure 4–2 is a pre-call preparation checklist.

As you prepare for your face-to face meeting, review your research for possible missed clues to service needs. From your initial phone conversations, you'll have an idea of what the prospect needs. Now you can prioritize service areas and identify gaps in your research. Then you'll know what you must accomplish at the meeting. If you prepare for the sales call, you'll find that your confidence level will increase tremendously. Ask any successful accountant and they will tell you that planning and structure builds confidence. And isn't confidence what most of us lack, the confidence that we will be successful in developing new business? We cannot overemphasize the importance of pre-call

FIGURE 4–1
A Simplified Sales Call Plan

Company _____
Person   Title
Phone _____
Receptionist _____
Last call date_____
Results _____

Objectives for Personal Sales Call
1. _____
2. _____
3. _____

Opening Statement (Eliminates nervousness)

_____
_____

Possible Probe Questions for Need Identification (linked to your research about firm)

_____
_____

Key Benefits and Features you will stress (allows you to have correct materials on hand)

_____
_____

Predicted Objections

_____
_____

Applicable Close Techniques

_____
_____
_____

Source: David A. Reid, *The Sales Presentation Manual* (St. Paul, MN: West Publishing Company, 1992).

FIGURE 4–2
Pre-Call Preperation Checklist

For each item listed below, make sure you can check off a yes. Nos highlight areas that can cause you to lose a sale.

	Yes	No
• Confirmed appointment with right person.		
• Know names, titles, and pronunciations.		
• Know purpose of call.		
• Client needs known to date.		
• Know client's objectives.		
• Know prime advantages of my product/service.		
• Anticipated client's possible responses.		
• Have I adopted my approach to the client's style?		
• Organized file for quick reference if needed.		
• Organized briefcase.		
• Documents and papers arranged in good order.		
• Brochures and other literature clean and up-to-date.		
• Presentation manual clean and unmarked.		
• Notebook and business cards readily available.		
• Support materials ready—samples, graphics.		
• Consider time available and material.		
• Consider commitment that I expect and keys to receiving a positive response.		

Source: Jack Greening, *Selling Without Confrontation* (Binghamton, NY: Haworth Press, 1993), p. 26.

planning. It is the only opportunity you may have to plan your strategy. If you've done your research and demonstrate that you know the prospect's industry and the problems he or she faces, your initial talks can immediately focus on specific service needs and possible solutions.

WHAT YOU NEED TO KNOW ABOUT YOUR PROSPECT'S INDUSTRY

To successfully attract business, you must have a solid grasp of your prospect's industry. At a minimum, you should be aware of:

- Trends and key buzz words in the industry.
- Profitability of leading companies in the industry.
- Your prospect's main competitors and suppliers.
- Any special accounting or tax rules in the industry.

Some of your most valuable sources of information are within your firm. Read reports on engagements your firm has performed for other companies in the industry. Meet with those who worked on those engagements. Check financial statements to get a grip on the fiscal realities of the industry. Your referral network can help, too. Lending officers often have unique insights into financial issues facing an industry. If you have an acquaintance or firm alumni working for the prospect or another firm in the industry, their opinions can be valuable.

Outside your firm, there also are a number of good sources. These are all readily available and for the most part free. Any good library will have the following sources:

- Standard & Poor's Industry Surveys

  U.S. Industrial Outlook published annually by the U.S. Department of Commerce

  Industry Trade Associations' surveys
- Trade and Industry journals

In addition, the major brokerage houses have industry studies that are readily available. Use *Nelson's Directory of Wall Street Reasearch.*

WHAT YOU NEED TO KNOW
ABOUT YOUR PROSPECT'S COMPANY

It's also important to learn what you can about your prospect's/client's company. However, this information is mostly for background. When you do contact the client, let them tell you about themselves. They know their company best. While they'll appreciate your taking the time to learn about them and their industry, they won't appreciate someone who acts as if he or she knows more about their operations than they do. Still, there are things you should know. Check the local and trade press to see if the prospect has been in the news. If they recently opened a new plant, expanded their offices, or introduced a new product, you should be prepared to discuss it. Again, your referral network is valuable. The person who gave you the referral may have considerable knowledge about the company and its needs. Dun & Bradstreet or other credit reporting agencies can give insight into their financial health. *Standard & Poor's Regester of Corporation, Moody's Manuals and News Reports,* and *MacMillan Directory of Leading Private Companies* are three key sources you should consult.

WHAT YOU NEED TO KNOW ABOUT YOUR PROSPECT'S DECISION MAKERS

As part of the qualification process, you identified the decision makers at your prospect's company. Try to learn their titles and the organizational structure of the company. *Who's Who* directories, company literature, such as annual reports and proxy statements and various other directories such as *Dun's Reference Book of Corporate Management Standard & Poor's Register of Executives* frequently offer this information. These publications also contain valuable personal details. Perhaps the prospect's CFO attended your alma mater. Maybe he's listed as head of a local amateur golf outing or United Way campaign. Such details can be a big help in building and cementing the relationships that are so important when selling and providing services.

WHAT YOU NEED TO KNOW ABOUT YOUR SERVICES

Here's an important step many professionals skip. "I know my services," they say. They're right—and they're wrong. You certainly know your services from a technical perspective. You can explain what they are and how they're performed. But can you clearly explain the benefits the prospect can expect? Can you succinctly show how your firm can help increase your prospect's profitability and efficiency? Are you prepared to answer objections concerning fees? Can you readily answer the question "Why buy from us?" Draft benefit statements for the services you sell. These statements should stress the benefit of the service to the buyer. For instance, suppose you want to recommend establishing a profit-sharing plan to a prospect with high taxes and high employee turnover. Your benefit statement could be as follows:

> A profit-sharing plan lets you use earnings that currently go to taxes to benefit your employees. By giving workers a piece of the action, you can expect better productivity and lower turnover. And, since plan contributions are deductible, you'll recognize sizable tax savings.

While this statement doesn't address the technical details of establishing a profit-sharing plan, it clearly summarizes for the prospect some of the benefits a plan offers. That generates interest. Armed with a qualified prospect, a solid grounding in the concerns the company faces, and a clearly articulated list of benefits the prospect can expect from your firm, you're ready for the meeting.

Chapter Five

If You Want to Sell, Listen

"Whenever two people are talking, no one is listening."

Anonymous

INTRODUCTION

We have only one goal for this chapter: We want to teach you the importance of listening. That is the only way you will learn about your prospect's needs. There is an old saying that "God gave us two ears and one mouth for a very good reason." Some might say that we should listen twice as much as we speak. When it comes to learning about your clients' and potential clients' needs, you really need to be listening 80 or 90 percent of the time and speaking only 10 or 20 percent. It may be good to remember another wise saying: "You can't hear what someone else is saying when you are speaking." Yet, most of us want to speak instead of listen. This major fault in selling will cost many sales.

Listening is a skill that each and every one of us can develop. It's no different than developing the skills that have made you a great tax advisor or accountant. First, you need to understand what you have to learn. Then, you learn it. Finally, you practice it so that it becomes second nature. We have found that the most successful accountants are those who have honed their listening skills. If there is one secret for success that you need to remember it is this: Those who listen best are those who identify concerns and build relationships with others. As Tom Peters noted in *Thriving on Chaos,* to learn this skill you need to spend time in the marketplace, listen with intensity, take what you heard seriously, and act quickly. (Peters, Tom. *Thriving on Chaos,* New York: Kopt, 1987, pp. 434–440.)

SELF ASSESSMENT 5–1:
YOUR COMMUNICATIONS IQ

The following series of questions is a tool for self-assessment of your current listening and communicating skills. These statements are adapted from a test of Communications IQ prepared by William M. Sattler, Department of Speech, University of Michigan.

Directions: Please note the number that *generally* applies to you.

Speech

Very Seldom	Once in a while	Occasionally	Fairly Often	Almost Always
1	2	3	4	5

1. I look at the person I am talking with.
2. I do *not* do other things (arrange papers, sign letters, etc.) while I am talking with the person.
3. I plan my message before delivering it.
4. I explain *why* a new policy, method, and so on, is to be followed.
5. I follow up to see if instructions, orders, methods, and so on, were carried out.
6. I explain to the individual the impact of the message.

Attitudes

Very Seldom	Once in a while	Occasionally	Fairly Often	Almost Always
1	2	3	4	5

1. I use the person's name I am talking with.
2. I show respect toward the person I am talking with.
3. I welcome advice, suggestions, constructive criticism, and so on from others.
4. I praise subordinates and peers when their work deserves it.
5. I like to talk to all subordinates; I don't play favorites.

Language and Thought

Very Seldom	Once in a while	Occasionally	Fairly Often	Almost Always
1	2	3	4	5

1. I am aware of when I am reporting facts and when I am making inferences.

2. I am aware of the differences between observed phenomena and inferences or judgments.
3. I am aware that what I say is often conditioned by my own inner state: my feelings, emotions, and prejudices.
4. I itemize points *pro* and *con* rather than oversimplify by expressing sweeping generalizations (everybody, always).
5. I picture the world of the person I am speaking to: his or her frame of reference, situation, and environment.
6. I refrain from excessive redundancy and repetition by permitting the person to translate my message into his or her own words.

Listening after Message Sending

Very Seldom	Once in a while	Occasionally	Fairly Often	Almost Always
1	2	3	4	5

1. I give the person a chance to ask questions.
2. I invite the person to restate my message if he or she wishes to do so.
3. I do not disagree with the person until I fully understand his or her idea or point of view.
4. Before I disagree, I show in what respect I agree with the person.

Situation

Very Seldom	Once in a while	Occasionally	Fairly Often	Almost Always
1	2	3	4	5

1. I try to listen to subordinates and others in a quiet place that is free from distractions.
2. I am willing to listen to others in informal on-the-job situations as well as in planned conferences or interviews.
3. When I do not fully understand,I say, "Talk again on that point."
4. I restate the other person's point of view to their satisfaction; for example, "Your point is... You mean that..."
5. I don't let emotionally toned words affect my behavior.

6. I listen not only to facts and ideas but also to the feelings the person reveals.

7. I also ask questions to be sure I have received the message correctly.

8. I try not make the other person feel that he or she is inferior to me.

9. I'll change my ideas after listening if facts point to the wisdom of the change.

10. I feel subordinates and peers feel as free to give me adverse reports as favorable reports.

Once you have completed the above self-assessment, pick out those questions in each section where you scored a "1" or "2." These are definite areas for you to work on and improve. After you have covered these areas, you should look at the questions for which you gave yourself a "3." These also need to be reviewed and worked on. We recommend that you also let someone else evaluate your listening skills. Give them a copy of this assessment and ask them to rate you. This will give you some idea of how you are perceived. If their answers and yours are very close, you have an accurate self-impression. However, if they are far apart, how you see yourself and how the outside world sees you may be quite different.

LISTENING: A TWO-WAY COMMUNICATION

The next step in the listening process is to gain an understanding of what you need to do to become an effective listener. As we mentioned earlier, the most important part of bringing in new business is identifying what the prospect or client needs. Effective salespeople are great listeners. Here's what you will need to know to become a great listener and effective new business developer: Listening is really a two-way, not one-way, communication; active listening is the key to making sales.

Since nearly half of the communication process takes place with the receiver of the message, it is important to understand the art of listening as well as that of speaking. If we blame a fellow associate or a potential client for miscommunication by saying, "You weren't paying attention," we are abdicating our responsibility as speakers.

J. Campbell Connelly, in *A Manager's Guide to Speaking and Listening,*[1] lists nine listening "traps" to avoid. He suggests that all nine of these traps result from what he considers the "only bad listening habit: *mind-wandering.*" As we will see, listening is hard work, and we need to be careful not to lapse into a subconscious state of listening lethargy. How many of these listening traps do you associate yourself with?

1. **Considering the subject uninteresting.** We all possess a mental "censor" which, if not controlled, will affect our attention to the speaker. This censor will cause us to pay less attention to subjects we may not consider interesting and more attention to subjects we consider interesting, though perhaps less important. Therefore, it is important to remember that the prospect, client, or referral source must have something important to say to us when we are involved in a conversation. We should pay attention regardless of our estimation of the speaker.

2. **Evaluating the speaker instead of the message.** We have all been guilty of falling into this trap: We know that Robert is ostentatious, so we only listen to half of what he says; we dislike Janet, so we deliberately tune out her message. The technique to use here is to close out those aspects of the speaker's personality that are distracting and concentrate on the message.

3. **Becoming emotionally involved.** The speaker may say something that offends us. But if we become emotionally involved during the communication, chances are we will never receive the message clearly. It is better for us to hold emotion in check until after we have received and understood the message. This way, we can base our response on correct information.

4. **Listening only for facts.** More than just facts are presented during a conversation. As in the adage, "Not being able to see the forest for the trees," by concentrating on the specific facts in a message, we are prone to miss the ideas. We were once working with a small business owner who called us in to help him with his marketing. He began by giving us a lot of facts about declining sales, lower profit margins, and so on. But behind the facts were other words that led us to believe that he was interested in more than just improving his marketing effectiveness. His main idea was to sell the business within a

---

[1]Adapted from J. Campell Connelly, *A Manager's Guide to Speaking and Listening.* New York, NY: American Management Association, 1967. pp. 55–67.

few years. Believe us, if had only been focusing on the facts, we would never have picked up this other aspect of the conversation. Because our schooling taught us to listen for facts so we would be prepared for examinations, few people are able to spot the main idea in a presentation or conversation. Thus, we must listen clearly and communicate back to the speaker in order to gain a full understanding of what is being said.

5. **Taking copious notes.** Excessive note taking is one of the surest ways of not getting what the speaker says. It is impossible to write down everything the speaker says without reducing the communication to a snail's pace. Many of us have tried to communicate with someone who takes notes while we are speaking and found they had difficulty grasping what had been said. While they were writing down what we said, they did not have time to think about what was being said.

6. **Feigning attention.** Most of us can remember doing this in school and in other learning situations. Whether due to fatigue or complexity of the communication, we resort to this technique. It now can occur subconsciously during our workdays; should we begin to daydream on the job, our physical self will maintain a posture of attention.

7. **Letting yourself be distracted.** We can be distracted in two ways: physically and mentally. We may be distracted by a fly in the room or by the boss's speech impediment. Or we may be distracted by other tangential thoughts, possibly inspired by the ideas that are being communicated. As a result, we may distract ourselves and others by interrupting and digressing, taking the communication away from its intended direction. As in trap (3) we must discipline ourselves to wait until we digest the entire communication before discussing it.

8. **Avoiding difficult listening.** Some of us hear but do not listen. Because we have never developed good listening skills, we have difficulty with messages that are extremely detailed or abstract. Like the adult who still reads only the comic strips and the sports page, relying on television for news, we have avoided situations where the language or specifics might take us into deep concentration. To avoid this trap, develop expertise in difficult areas, learning, for instance, the technical jargon necessary to accurately discuss a situation relevant to your work. For example, if you are not technically oriented, gain enough knowledge to be able to discuss the use of a local area network (LAN) or preparing a tax return on Windows.

9. **Reacting to loaded words.** Loaded words are a speaker's nemesis because they can trigger a reaction that completely disrupts the communication process. Every listener has developed his or her own unique set of volatile words and expressions. For example, there are certain topics today that seem to be extremely sensitive. You wouldn't want to get into a discussion with a prospect about being "politically correct" without at least knowing where the individual stood on the subject. Everyone has their own set of words; you need to be able to read the other person's reactions to your conversation.

Verbal communication involves both speaking and listening. Since the success of the communication is the speaker's responsibility, we must have a full grasp of the entire process and understand how and why a listener may have difficulty receiving the message. With an understanding of these listening "traps," you are now prepared to prevent them from happening.

EMPATHY: A MAJOR PART OF LISTENING

When we send out a message, it is important for us to empathize, or put ourselves in the receiver's shoes. This is the only way we can be relatively certain that our message will be understood. Conversely, as listeners, we need to empathize in order to determine if there may be a hidden message that the speaker is trying to convey. For example, a speaker making a simple request may be actually trying to say, "I have a problem." By understanding their perspective, we may be able to help them communicate this message more clearly through two-way communication. A client once called us in to discuss a recent valuation of his business. The reason he was concerned about the valuation was not because he wanted to sell the business but because he needed a substantial loan and wanted to use this one business as the primary collateral. We are sure you can think of several situations in which you thought the client wanted one thing and in reality it turned out to be something else. When this happens, it is usually because we just didn't listen well enough, didn't give the prospect enough time to talk and articulate his or her real problems. To avoid this, remember these key techniques:

- Practice paying close attention to content and feeling of messages. We were once consulting with a lawyer who had not been home for dinner for over a month. During the course of our conversation we became aware of the imbalance between his personal and professional life. The cause of the problem was his fear of taking in a partner to help him with his work. We discussed some ways for him to protect his practice, hire an associate, and eventually be able to put more balance into his life. If we hadn't been paying attention to the content and feeling of the conversation, I don't think we would have gotten the engagement.

- Hold back on making judgments or determining what you want to say until you have fully listened and understood what is being said to you. You will know the minute you are not listening when you are already thinking of the answer while the other person is still talking.
- Verbally play back to the speaker what you heard; then probe to see if you have reached a deeper understanding of his or her position. This will indicate a high interest and support of the speaker's thinking.
- Paraphrase back to a person your perception of his or her viewpoint before stating your own viewpoint.
- Take notes. There is nothing wrong with taking a pen and paper into a meeting. You don't need to take down every word that is said. But it is critical to capture key ideas, goals, figures, and so on so that you can refer to this information at a later date when you are presenting your solution to the client's or prospect's problem. You can take down comments the prospect makes so you can remind him or her later of the benefits that you discussed. For example, a client might tell you exactly what he or she is trying to accomplish. Capturing the issue in the prospect's own words and repeating them in your follow-up letter can serve as a powerful reminder that you truly know what the prospect wants.
- Use body language to show the speaker you are interested in what he or she saying. Good eye contact, an alert look, an occasional "Yes, I see," will all give the prospect the indication that you are paying close attention.

LISTENING REQUIRES YOU LEARN
TO ASK QUESTIONS

Learning how to listen also requires that you ask the right questions. If you are listening, it is your responsibility to ask questions. If you find yourself speaking more than 20 percent of the time, you are not listening.

The minute you stop listening, you are no longer able to identify the needs of the prospect. When you are in the listening stage of the selling cycle, don't sell. As we define this stage, you are trying to identify the concerns, problems, and issues. Since you don't know what these are at this stage, how do you know what to offer?

If you are only going to be speaking 20 percent of the time, it is critical that you know what to ask the prospect. All you need to remember are five words:

- **How?** How did you first get started in this business? How did the business grow so fast?
- **When?** When did you find out that you were losing market share? When are you trying to finish the project?
- **Where?** Where do you want to open the new facilities? When you left your previous company, where did you go?
- **What?** What specifically do you want to accomplish if we do this project? What would be the timetable for this engagement? What didn't you like about your last accountant?
- **Why?** Why are you switching accounting firms now?

You will note that all the questions above require the respondent to give some explanation, not just a yes or no answer. There are basically two types of questions you can ask: open-ended and closed-ended. If you are trying to discover the prospect's needs, you will want to use as many open-ended questions as possible. You just need to remember that some open-ended questions may be too personal for the prospect to answer right away. You will want to build up to the more sensitive and personal questions, not begin your conversation with them. Let's look at some sample closed-ended and open-ended questions.

Closed-ended questions: Did you buy extra inventory yesterday? Are you going to sell the company this year?

Open-ended questions: Why did you buy extra inventory yesterday? What are your plans to sell the company?

CONTROL DISTRACTIONS

Another key element to effective listening is to control and reduce the amount noise in any important conversation. Noise can be defined as any distraction that takes place during the course of a conversation.

It can be people coming in and out of a restaurant, music in the background, a fire truck outside, phone calls, and so on. All of these small and not so small disturbances can distract you and your prospect from the real business at hand. When meeting a prospect in a restaurant, always take the seat against the wall so that the prospect can focus his or her attention on you and not on all the activity that is taking place in the restaurant. Here is a list of some other "noise" eliminators.

1. Make sure your phone is on forward when meeting with prospects and clients in your office.
2. Don't let anyone interrupt your meeting.
3. Meet in a conference room rather than in your office.
4. Keep the blinds or curtains closed so that you are not distracted by events outside of the office.

ACTIVE LISTENING

There is listening, and then there is active listening. As we have already said, to get the information you need, it's important to ask a lot of questions. It's even more important to listen effectively or actively. What is active listening? It's not only focusing on what the prospect is saying and looking for the meaning behind the words, it's also giving the prospect feedback about what you've heard. Active listening is not thinking ahead to what you're going to say. An active listening conversation might go like this:

You: Kate, this is what I believe you are saying. Your inventory turn is not as high as the industry average, and you don't know where the problem is.

Client: Well, that's not exactly what I was saying. You are right that my inventory turn is not as high as the industry average, but I do know what the problem is. I just don't know how to solve it. Let me explain what I mean....

Active listening will reveal how an individual feels about what's going on. Is he or she giving you one-word answers? You may be coming on too strong, and the prospect may be feeling defensive. We have found that few people are good natural listeners, even though we spend about 40 percent of our day in a listening mode. By listening carefully, you will be able to pick up important sales cues. Three especially helpful sales cues are personal motivation, service, and conversational cues. Let's look at each one separately.

Personal Motivation Cues

These cues tell you the personal objectives behind the decision-making process of the individual you're talking to. Does your prospect say things like, "It's important to establish who's the boss"? This tells you that this particular prospect needs to feel in control in most situations. Or what about this: "This is our last chance. If we don't make it this time, we're through." It is likely that security is a major factor in any decision this prospect makes.

Service Cues

Is the prospect using words like *improve, reduce, eliminate, protect, restructure,* or *identify*? If you hear such words, listen carefully, because the prospect is revealing to you a specific area of need. You can now begin to see the importance of developing your listening skills. Imagine that a prospect is interested in protecting his or her retirement investment, and you start to suggest a new risky solution to the problem. It's a pretty good bet you won't be selected to help that prospect out.

Conversational Cues

Conversational cues are a bit more difficult to identify. You will need to pay as much attention as possible to capture them. Say, for example, you ask the prospect: "What inventory controls do you have in place?" And she answers, "We've automated most of the system." You need to decide how to proceed. The prospect has not really answered your question. Should you continue the dialogue to obtain more general information about the company's inventory controls? Or should you ask a specific question to clarify what parts of the inventory system have been automated?

What is important is that you become aware of the types of cues (personal motivation, service, or conversational) that the prospect is giving you. Here's one more important tip: Let prospects talk as long as they want to even after they've answered one of your specific questions. They will provide you with additional information and bring up otherwise hidden needs or concerns.

TYPES OF FEEDBACK

Nonverbal Feedback

The most important thing you need to remember in developing your active listening skills is to focus on the prospect or client. This can be done in two ways. First, by using nonverbal feedback. Some of the more basic nonverbal expressions are as follows:

- Smile and face the prospect squarely. Tilting the head, placing your hand on your cheek, and stroking your chin are all nonverbal signs of evaluation.
- Open your posture. For example, keep your hands open, unbutton your coat, move closer to the client.
- Make positive movements, such as leaning forward, uncrossing your arms and legs. Nodding is also positive. Remember, drumming your fingers, swinging your legs, looking at your watch, fidgeting, and frowning are all negative expressions.
- Make eye contact. It is always better to look the prospect right in the eyes. You don't want to stare the prospect down, but you also don't want to be talking to the wall.
- Physical space is important. The social distance guide in the United States is 0–2 feet, intimate zone; 2–4 feet, personal zone; 4–12 feet, social zone. More than 12 feet, public zone. The safest space is usually between 4 and 5 feet unless you are asked to come closer.

Verbal Feedback

The second way to focus on the prospect is by using verbal feedback. You can use short supportive verbal comments, such as "Yes, I see," or "That's interesting." It's important to avoid inciting words that are emotionally active and that may produce a defensive stance with the prospect. Here is a list of phrases and topics you will want to stay away from:

- Do you see my point?

- You don't understand.
- See?
- Do you understand?
- Do you follow me?
- Are you aware of...?
- This is easy to understand, isn't it?
- References to religion, gender, race, ethnic background.
- References to sexual preferences.
- Vulgarity.
- Profanity.

Paraphrasing ideas as well as feelings is an important part of verbal feedback. Purchasing accounting and consulting services is a very personal thing. The business owner opens himself or herself up to financial scrutiny and performance. If you can identify the owner's true feelings, you will more often than not get the engagement. Paraphrasing is nothing more than feeding back to the prospect his or her ideas and feelings in order to get confirmation.

Finally there is one more way to make active listening effective. By using relational feedback; that is, adding a specific example from your own experience that relates to the prospect's comments. This comment may be personal or of a business nature. The purpose is to show the prospect you have a deep understanding of the issue because you have either helped others out or have had to resolve the same problem yourself. For example, as an owner of your accounting firm, we are sure there have been times when you had insufficient cash on hand to make payroll. Many small business owners have faced the same problem. By relating your experience to the prospect, you will form a mutual bond.

We have included several checklists as appendices. Use them as helpful reminders to improve your listening effectiveness. Appendix 5–1 provides you with 13 techniques to improve your listening skills. Appendix 5–2 provides you with cues to tell if the prospect is listening to you, and Appendix 5–3 will let you know if the prospect is not listening. You may want to photocopy these and keep them with you when making sales calls.

Note: For more information on relational feedback see Mary Ann Oberhaus, Sharon Ratliffe, and Vernon Stauble, *Professional Selling: A Relationship Process,* Fort Worth, TX. Harcourt, Brace College Publishers, 1993, p. 289.

Appendix 5–1
TECHNIQUES TO IMPROVE
YOUR LISTENING SKILLS

1. Limit your own talking. You can't talk and listen at the same time.

2. Think like the prospect. His problems and needs are important, and you'll understand and retain them better if you listen to his point of view.

3. Ask questions. If you don't understand something or feel you may have missed a point, clear it up now before it embarrasses you later.

4. Don't interrupt. A pause doesn't always mean a prospect has finished saying everything she wants to say.

5. Concentrate. Focus your mind on what the prospect is saying. Practice shutting out distractions.

6. Take notes. This will help you remember important points. But be selective. Trying to note everything a prospect says can result in being left far behind or retaining irrelevant details.

7. Listen for ideas. You want to get the whole picture, not just isolated bits and pieces.

8. Listen for overtones. You learn a great deal about the prospect from the way he reacts to the things you say.

9. An occasional, "Yes" or "I see" shows the speaker you are still with her, but don't overdo or use as a meaningless comment.

10. Turn off your own worries. This isn't always easy, but personal fears, worries, and problems not connected with the prospect form a kind of "static" that can block the prospect's message.

11. Prepare in advance. Remarks and questions prepared in advance free your mind for listening.

12. React to ideas only. Don't argue mentally. Don't allow the irritation at things the prospect may say or his manner distract you.

13. Don't jump to conclusions. Avoid making unwarranted assumptions about what the prospect is going to say or mentally try to complete her sentence for her.

Appendix 5–2
HOW TO TELL IF THE PROSPECT IS LISTENING

1. Looks you in the eyes.
2. Touches your hand or arm.
3. Leans toward you and smiles.
4. Has a pleasant facial expression.
5. Grins.
6. Faces you directly.
7. Nods affirmatively.
8. Licks lips.
9. Raises eyebrows.
10. Keeps eyes open wide.
11. Uses expressive hand gestures while speaking.

Appendix 5–3
HOW TO TELL IF THE PROSPECT IS NOT LISTENING

1. Stops talking.
2. Fidgets with pen or doodles.
3. Glances sideways.
4. Crosses hands on chest.
5. Leans away from you.
6. Sneers.
7. Yawns.
8. Frowns.
9. Looks at ceiling.
10. Shakes head negatively.
11. Cleans fingernails.
12. Cracks knuckles.
13. Jingles change or keys.

Source: Jack Greening, *Selling Without Confrontation*, Binghampton, NY: Hawthorn Press, 1993, p. 120–121 (Source for 5–2 and 5–3 only).

Chapter Six

Situational Selling:
The Secret to Understanding
Your Buyer

INTRODUCTION

In this chapter, we will show you how to understand different buyers and will take you through the stress-filled first meeting with a prospect. They say first impressions last a lifetime. In sales, it's especially true. Your confidence, competence, and demeanor at your first meeting can mean the difference between a new client or a lost prospect. Why? From the prospect's viewpoint, your attitude and performance directly reflect your firm and its ability to provide the prospect with a brighter (more profitable) future.

If at the start, you take on a consultative role and help the prospect make a good buying decision without feeling pressured, you will soon find yourself closing more and more business. By keeping the spotlight on the prospect, you will learn to identify what the prospect is looking for and how to deliver it. A prepared script or pushy sales pitch can only hurt your case. Remember to control the meeting by asking open-ended questions and by getting the information you need to identify the prospect's real needs, not just the symptoms of the problem.

Remember, no cold calls, either on the phone or in person! That's right; don't call first. Recall what we said in Chapter 4: Write first. Then call to make an appointment. Then follow up with a personal visit for the fact-finding phase of the selling cycle. Yes this is a lot of work, but the systematic approach is the most efficient and effective way. You should make a weekly plan of leads/prospects you will call to set up appointments and then keep a daily call log and weekly call log in which you record outcomes of these efforts. Accountants who sell are those who can best establish personal and business relationships with their

prospects. They not only understand the dynamics of interpersonal relationships, but they also know how to adapt their selling style to fit
the prospect.

SELF-ASSESSMENT 6–1: SITUATIONAL SELLING

The following self-assessment will tell you how much you know about
situational selling. Take a few minutes and answer each question true
or false. For each question you answer incorrectly, you should read the
corresponding section in this chapter.

1. Situational selling is a deceptive method of selling accounting
   services. T or F?
2. All buyers need to be treated in the same manner. T or F?
3. I can never learn how to read a buyer like a book. T or F?
4. A buyer's behavior can be observed in terms of two basic
   dimensions. T or F?
5. There are four basic personality types you meet in selling
   situations. T or F?

(Answer: 1 F; 2 F; 3 F; 4 T; 5 T)

UNDERSTANDING THE FIRST SALES CALL

The first sales call is obviously the most important. If you don't cut
the muster here, you won't have the opportunity to return for a second
visit. The first sales call can be divided into three main sections. The
first section is the opening. During this stage, you will want to introduce yourself and other team members and outline the main purpose
of the meeting. As we will see, depending on the type of personality
you are selling to, this opening stage of the sales call can dramatically
change. Later on in the chapter, we will give you some ideas on how
to sell to different personality types.

Once you get beyond the opening stage, you will want to move into
the second section of the sales call. In this stage, you are trying to discover the prospect's needs. You will do this by asking questions, listening, summarizing the needs, and answering any objections that are
raised. The third section is the conclusion of the sales call. There are
two ways the initial sales call may end. One, you ask for and get the

business. Two, and most likely, you will have to come back, probe more, and develop the relationship with the prospect. Above all, you don't want to leave the first meeting without some specific next action step. For example, you may call back in two weeks, have your tax partner get in contact with the prospect, and so on.

THE ADAPTIVE SELLING METHOD

Successful selling requires as many skills as being a successful auditor. Perhaps the most important skills an accountant can learn are interpersonal skills. Unfortunately, most accountants have had little or no training in this area. Sellers of accounting and tax-related services today meet a variety of prospects. The key to being a successful salesperson is the seller's ability to adapt himself or herself to a variety of personalities. It is critical for you to learn how to adapt your personal style to match that of your prospect. To be successful at sales, it is important that you do not react to a prospect's behavior with your own set of reactions. Let's give a short example. The prospect is the type of person who likes to talk and really get to know the people he or she is going to work with. You are the type of person who is always in a hurry and just want to get the job done. If you act the way you normally would, do you think this prospect will feel comfortable with you and want to do business with you? We doubt it!

The key to making more sales is to understand each buyer and how he or she works. This is called the adaptive or situational selling method and has been used successfully by professional salespeople in many different industries, especially in the financial services industries. The adaptive selling method is based on these concepts:

- Prospects buy services for their reasons, not yours.
- The prospect's agenda is often different from yours.
- Prospects will expect you to act a certain way. If these expectations are not met, the buyer feels mistrust and retreats.
- Each prospect is unique; therefore, your approach needs to be unique.

When you start thinking from the prospect's point of view, you begin to realize that going into a selling situation, the prospect has fears and concerns. You may represent change for the prospect that she or he is not yet ready for. For example, you may be suggesting to a father that his son or daughter take over the business. The prospect doesn't know you and may be wondering if you can be trusted. For example, you are helping a prospect with developing an estate plan and are making suggestions that he or she give a sizeable gift to the children and other relatives. Or you may suggest that the prospect place their money with a certain investment house. If the prospect does not have a lot of experience with you, you can imagine what's going through his or her head. Finally, the prospect may be wondering if the entire meeting is worth his or her time. The prospect could well be thinking, "Why not just leave everything as it is?"

These types of questions must be addressed and often answered in the first sales call if the sales process is to move forward. Our experience has been that most accountants do not give enough thought to the buyer. They are so concerned about impressing the prospect that they far too often fail to hear, see, or feel what the prospect really needs and wants.

UNDERSTANDING YOUR PROSPECT'S PERSONALITY

In order to understand prospects, you need to listen to what they say and watch how they are saying it and what they do. Don't worry about anything else: a hidden agenda, your own fears, or problems of the day. Concentrate all you energies on the buyer. You can pick up on the prospect's signals by paying attention to his or her language. Does the prospect use words such as *picture* or *focus* (visual words)? Does a particular idea "strike a chord" or "ring a bell" (auditory images)? Or does a statement "rub him the wrong way" (physical descriptors)? Once you recognize the type of language the prospect uses, build it into your sales vocabulary. You can also match your sales style to the prospect's perceptual system. Is the prospect visually oriented? If so, use charts and draw diagrams. If auditory, use interesting narrative. Physical? Ask for a tour of his facilities so you can get a "feeling" for the operation.

You will also want to focus your energies on your prospect's behavior. You want to make sure that your perception of your prospect's behavior is accurate. Behavior can be assessed in terms of two observable dimensions: assertiveness and responsiveness. In The Versatile Salesperson course, Wilson Learning Corporation defines assertiveness as "the way in which a person is perceived as attempting to influence the thoughts and actions of others." Obviously, there are different methods of assertiveness. Not all buyers are the same. The assertiveness scale ranges from ask-assertive at one end to tell-assertive at the other. The assertiveness range helps us pinpoint where a particular prospect might be. Prospects who fall to the far left (ask-assertive) will ask a lot of questions before making up their minds. Prospects to the far right (tell-assertive) are much more direct; rather than ask questions, they make statements to control the situation. They take risks and are fast paced in the actions and decisions.

The other behavior characteristic that you need to become aware of is responsiveness. This is an important characteristic since it will tell you how interested the buyer is in the personal aspects of the sales situation. Responsiveness is defined as the way in which a person is perceived as expressing emotions when relating to others. This dimension of human behavior will tell you how emotionally open or closed the prospect is. The responsiveness scale runs from top to bottom. At the top is task-directed (i.e., facts), and at the bottom is people-directed (i.e., emotions). People at the top are focused on the task. They will stick to business topics. Those at the bottom are more likely to want to spend time talking and getting to know you on a personal as well as professional level. You can imagine how far you will get trying to be casual and friendly with a prospect who by nature is formal and reserved.

The Versatile Salesperson program is based on the premise that, by observing ways of assertiveness and responsiveness in others, you can identify buyers as belonging to one of four social styles. We strongly believe that this is a most effective way of understanding your prospect's personality; it's easy to understand, and above all it's easy to use. We suggest that you first identify your own style. Knowing that will take you a long way towards becoming comfortable with what we are discussing. Many accountants tell us that they feel as if they are being deceptive with the client by adapting a style that is not really their own. This process does not require you to be deceptive. Rather, you are trying to behave in a manner that will make the client feel more comfortable. Many psychologists tell us that, in order to effectively communicate with another, we sometimes need to mirror their behavior and emotions.

Perhaps the following example will clarify what we are discussing. You are called by a client who is upset because the new computer system you just installed is always crashing. Instead of act-ing with a great degree of urgency, you merely tell the client to calm down and stop worrying. How do you think the client will react to your response? Now if you were to mirror the client's emotional state and say, "This sounds critical, I'll be right out there with our computer support team," do you think you would get a different response from the client? What's different in the second scenario? You read the emotional state of the client and reflected it back. Were you being deceptive? Of course not.

RESPONSIVENESS/ASSERTIVENESS MATRIX

By combining these two dimensions, you will be able to create the following grid that will be helpful in determining how best to adapt to the individual expectations of your prospects. This matrix is what Wilson Learning Corporation calls the Social Style Matrix. Through your observations of the prospect's behavior, you can determine their social style. You will soon be able to quickly place your clients and prospects into one of the four quadrants in Figure 6–1.

The Analytical Style

These people tend to be task-directed responsive and ask-assertive. The following gives some idea of their general characteristics:

- Detail oriented, deliberate, and well-organized.
- Listen carefully to information.
- Consider established policies, criteria, and objectives in making decisions.
- Tend to be selective about personal involvement with salespeople and let others take the social initiative.
- Prefer an efficient, businesslike sales approach.
- Practical and conservative in their business decisions.
- Tend to avoid uncomfortable situations by changing the subject or withdrawing from the salesperson.

Source: Reprinted by permission of Wilson Learning Corporation, *The Versatile Salesperson Reference Handbook*, p. 19.

FIGURE 6–1
Social Style Matrix

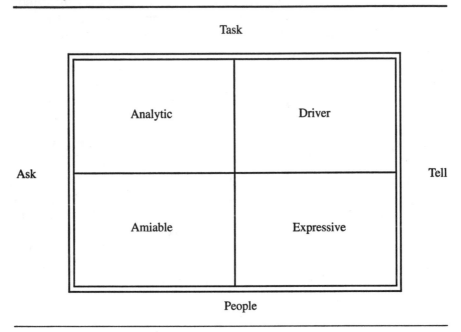

Task

| Analytic | Driver |

Ask   Tell

| Amiable | Expressive |

People

Source: Reprinted by permission of Wilson Learning Corporation. *The Versatile Salesperson.*

Here's an example of how you would sell to this type of prospect. First, make sure that prior to going to the meeting, you gather the information you will need to present and present it in a systematic way. If you don't do this, your meeting won't get very far. This buyer needs information. Therefore, you will need to provide sufficient information about your firm, the services you offer, and other supporting credentials. A brief slide show or handout material would be just fine with this type of prospect. If your buyer is the analytical type, don't expect a decision right away. You will need to allow adequate time for the prospect to process your information and recommendations. You should also be prepared to let this prospect have some additional time to think during your conversations. You won't be getting rapid responses from the analytical person. Don't jump in with another idea just because there is a pause in the conversation. Following some of these general ideas will make your sales call more successful.

The Driving Style

As the name implies, this is a fast-paced, hard-hitting individual. This buyer is perceived as task-directed responsive and tell-assertive. You will sell to this individual in a completely different manner than you did to the analytical prospect. Here are some of the general characteristics of the driver personality:

- Direct and to the point, showing little outward emotion.
- Confident, forceful, and results oriented.
- Tends to have a high sense of task urgency and little need for establishing relationships with salespeople.
- Has clear objectives and responds to salespeople who can demonstrate that their products or services can effectively achieve results.
- Keeps the discussion focused on objectives.
- Wants to be told of options and provided with probabilities of success.
- Wants a salesperson to listen carefully before recommending sales solutions.
- Attempts to balance cost and quality considerations when making decisions.
- Acts quickly after careful consideration of options

You will sell to the driver with a different style. Here's an example. Let's say you are calling on the managing partner of one of the larger and more aggressive law firms in your community. She has called you in to find out if you can help the firm become more profitable. Through your initial research and conversations with your referral sources, you have identified this individual as a driver. Once you are face to face with this prospect, you will quickly want to get down to business. Here is what you would do to make this sales call a success. You will want to gather the information about the project in an organized manner; since the driver is direct and to the point, she won't want to spend a lot of time. If you are going to close this sale, you will have to do timely follow-up. If you don't deliver on these promises, you won't get the engagement. The driver has a high sense of urgency. A slow follow-up will only tell her

---

Source: Reprinted by permission of Wilson Learning Corporation, *The Versatile Salesperson Reference Handbook,* p. 21.

that you are not interested in servicing her firm's needs on a timely basis. You are more likely to make this sale if you provide this driver with case histories, references, and factual supporting material. Selling to drivers requires that you have testimonial letters from satisfied clients, reprints of articles that you wrote or were written about your firm, documented results of similar types of profit improvement engagements, and so on. Finally, drivers like to receive options, not just one solution to a problem. The driver knows that there is more than one way to skin a cat and wants you to tell her the various ways to do it.

The Expressive Style

This buyer, as noted in the Figure 6–3 is perceived as tell-assertive and people-directed responsive. The expressive buyer will generally have these characteristics:

- Fast-paced, outgoing, and enthusiastic.
- Tends to be direct and open, even in uncomfortable situations.
- Innovative, willing to take risks.
- Shares her or his vision of the future; responsive to salespeople who will help achieve that vision.
- Concerned about the quality of solutions and their implementation.
- Takes time to establish open, trusting relations with those who can help achieve their goals.
- Wants to see the big picture before probing for details.
- Openly offers information to help salespersons meet needs.
- Motivating; attempts to enlist involvement of others.

If you find yourself selling to this personality type, follow the ideas suggested in the following example. You are meeting with the president of a high-tech start-up company. The company is developing voice recognition software. He has called you in to help with a computer systems problem. Unlike the driver, our buyer in this case will want to share with you his vision of where the company is going. You will have to listen and question attentively during these moments of the sales call. It will be important for you to demonstrate your competence

---

Source: Reprinted by permission of Wilson Learning Corporation, *The Versatile Salesperson Reference Handbook,* p. 23.

by citing other similar engagements or by having testimonial letters that you can show to the prospect. This buyer wants to develop a relationship from the start with those who can help him. One way of doing this is to enlist his involvement and input into the proposed solutions. Failure on your part to do so will surely result in an unsuccessful sales call. The expressive buyer will want to obtain internal support for the proposal at hand; you will need to explain or show him how to can gain such support. It may be support from a business associate or someone outside of the organization, such as a spouse or child. These other individuals may well be at your first sales call. Make sure you treat them with the same respect as the owner of the company. Finally, similar to the driver, the expressive buyer is not only concerned about follow-up but about the quality of the solutions and their implementation; it will be important to stay on top of the implementation process. If you fail here, you won't be called back for another engagement.

The Amiable Style

These are buyers who are ask-assertive and people-directed responsive. One side of them will be warm, spontaneous, and friendly (the people-responsive side); the other side will be cooperative and slow paced and will ask questions and suggest things (the ask-assertive side). When you identify the following characteristics in your prospects, you will know you are dealing with the amiable buyer:

- Open and sharing in relationships.
- Warm, cooperative, and deliberate but careful in business situations.
- Gathers and processess information with others; relies on shared decision making.
- Sensitive to the needs of others in the buying process.
- Wants to establish a strong trusting relationship with a salesperson before considering a purchase.
- Wants to feel assured that the services offered will be accepted by the organization.
- Wants to be assured that the buying decision will be supported by others and that the salesperson is a firm keeper of commitments.

Source: Reprinted by permission of Wilson Learning Corporation, *The Versatile Salesperson Reference Handbook*, p. 25.

Selling to the amiable buyer may test your patience. The most important thing you can do with this type of buyer is establish a trusting relationship. Although this buyer is warm and friendly, you may need to take some additional time in developing the relationship. Once you have a solid relationship developed, you may have a client for life. Your primary purpose at the initial sales call is to build the foundation for future calls. This can be done mainly by identifying mutual contacts and similar organizations that both of you belong to and by getting others in his or her firm to support you and your firm. You will need to meet the gatekeepers, users, and influencers in the buying decision. You will need to take time to understand the needs of the buyer and the other people in the organization.

Now that you realize there are different types of buyers with different personalities, we think you can begin to appreciate that successful sales calls just don't happen.* The next chapter will provide you with the information you will need to properly present yourself and begin the fact-finding and probing analysis portion of the sales cycle.

---

* To really become proficient at situational selling, we strongly recommend you attend the Wilson Learning Corporation training seminar. The time and money invested will well be worth your effort. Wilson Learning Corporation, 7500 Flying Cloud Drive, Eden Prairie, MN 55344. (612) 944-2880.

Chapter Seven

Finding the Hot Buttons: Fact-Finding and Probing Skills

INTRODUCTION

Imagine you are going to a doctor. Close your eyes for a minute and place yourself seated at the end of the examination table. The doctor begins to ask you several questions about your health and actually begins to poke his fingers here and there. Since your eyes are closed, you may not feel totally comfortable with what is going on. That is how prospects often feel when we start asking sensitive questions about the health of their business or personal financial health. Developing a keener sensitivity in this area will take you far as a professional advisor and problem solver.

This chapter will help you develop your fact-finding and probing skills. As you will see, they are part art and part science. The only way you will become proficient at these skills is through practice. We often recommend that you practice the skills you are learning now with your children, spouse, and others. So go ahead and practice as much as you can. This way, when you need to use these skills in business situations, you will feel comfortable and confident.

You have learned that you need to go the first meeting armed with listening skills and knowing how to identify prospect types. In addition, you have done your homework about the company and have basic information. Now it's time to really probe and find out what this prospect needs and wants. All too often, accountants fail at this critical stage because they are so sure they know better than anyone else, including the prospect, what the prospect really wants. If you ever catch yourself thinking this way, you'll know you have not yet learned how to listen or to use our *CPA* method to selling your services.

SELF ASSESSMENT 7–1: FACT FINDING AND PROBING

This assessment will give you some idea of your current fact-finding and probing skills and attitudes. Answer each statement yes or no.

1. Prior to the meeting I prepare a list of questions.
2. I know the difference between open-ended and closed-ended questions.
3. I could now create at least seven different types of open-ended questions.
4. I don't need to probe with prospects; I already know what they need and want.
5. I realize that probing is a two-way street and that the prospect wants to know something about me and my firm, too.

(Answers: You should have answered all questions yes, with the exception of question 4.)

THE OPENING STATEMENT

It's important to set the stage for the fact-finding phrase of the selling cycle. You don't want the prospect to feel uncomfortable, so you need to spend some time developing common ground. You are also trying to find out what type of personality your prospect is. Fact-finding really begins with your opening statement. Therefore, it is important to plan your opening statement in advance. Don't wait until you are in the meeting to start thinking about what you are going to say. Opening statements should be interesting. Depending on the situation, you might refer to a recent event that everyone can relate to. For example, you know that a major competitor in your prospect's industry has just suffered a decline in profits and sales. You could start your opening statement this way: "That was sure news last week when ABC Company announced it was laying off 200 people because of poor sales. What's that you're reading?" Or you can use a personal experience or anecdote that relates to the topic of the meeting. There are some basic elements of an opening statement that you should, of course, always include:

- **Your name and your role.** If there is more than one person from your firm at the meeting, make sure you introduce everyone and explain why they are there.

- **A statement that expresses the purpose of the meeting.** Often, this will come after the opening statement and often goes like this: "We really appreciate the opportunity to meet today and discuss your needs for business and tax advisory services. We are very interested in learning more about them and getting a clearer picture of what you want to accomplish."
- **A discussion lead-in or question.** The first question is really to get the ball rolling. You won't want it to be too penetrating or ask for personal or confidential information at this point. The best lead-in question is one that is broad in nature and will get the prospect talking more in generalities. For example, if you are aware of some changes taking place in the prospect's industry, you could ask him or her to further explain how these changes are having an impact on their business.

Figure 7–1 lists 22 types of fact-finding questions that represent the type of questions you will want to ask at a sales meeting.

ANSWERING THE PROSPECT'S QUESTIONS

The first meeting is a fact-finding interview not only for you but for the prospect as well. Remember, it is the prospect who has the problem. Even though you will initially want to direct your questions at more clearly defining his or her problem, you will have to answer some of the prospect's questions. Since most business owners enjoy talking about their company, ask for a brief history. This will go far toward breaking the ice and will also help you fill in your information gaps. But while all this is going on, remember, the prospect is trying to find the firm that's right for the company. The prospect will ask some fairly direct questions. You can avoid the most basic ones by starting the meeting with a brief introduction of your firm. But keep it short. Defer specific questions regarding services until you have the information you need. Tactfully answer questions on service, expertise, fees, and other matters but avoid selling or jeopardizing your firm's position until you've exactly defined the prospect's needs. Try to identify the motivation for each question. For example, a prospective client may ask about the size of your firm. A simple question, right? Maybe, but don't be too quick to answer. Instead, find out why this is important. If you answer without knowing the reason for the question, you may not have the proper perspective.

FIGURE 7–1
22 Fact Finding Questions

Use the following to generate thoughts and/or dialogue to focus your strategy with your prospect on the first call(s).

1. What major issues, opportunities, or problems may be confronting this industry or this company?
2. What are the company's recent financial results? Is there any trend or indicator that suggests a possible need?
3. Is there anything unusual, special, or unique about any item on the company's financial statement?
4. What does the financial statement tell us about the company? Is an opportunity indicated?
5. What questions should be asked of the company about its financial statement (for clarification or to demonstrate our expertise)?
6. What is known about the company's plans for the future? Do they suggest a possible need?
7. Who are the company's customers? Does anything about them indicate an opportunity with this company?
8. What technical accounting or tax issues may be involved in servicing this company? Do we have the required expertise?
9. What are our credentials in this industry?
10. Who are the company's current accountants? What do we know (or suspect) about their service to, or their relationship with, this company? What are their vulnerabilities?
11. What is the company looking for from its next accounting or consulting firm?
12. Who are the company's management/owners? Do we know any personally?
13. Who are the company's bankers, attorneys, underwriters or other professional relationships? Do any of these have relationships with us?
14. If so, what can these professionals tell us about the company's plans, operations, problems, and so on?
15. What will the decision process be? Who appears to be the decision maker(s) in the company? Do we know this person? Do our contacts know this person?
16. What additional information do we need about this company? Where can it be obtained? Who will obtain it? When?
17. What services are appropriate based on the needs of this company?
18. What appropriate references do we have?
19. What aspects of service should be emphasized with this company?
20. What objections are likely to be raised by the company? What will our response be?
21. Who should attend the meeting? What will be the respective roles?
22. Should we take and leave any materials? What?

Source: *Five Steps To New Client,* Chicago, IL: Practice Development Institute, 1990, printed with permission.

For example, suppose the prospect asks, "Is it true that you're the auditor for most of our competition?" Ask a question to clarify the prospect's concern, "Is your concern confidentiality?"

If the prospect affirms, you can reply, "It's true we have several clients in your industry. This gives us extensive expertise, so we can provide a higher level of service. However, we have a strict policy of confidentiality with all our clients."

PROBING MADE SIMPLE

What you have just experienced is a probing exercise. Probing is an effective questioning technique. It is a skill that will take you far in the selling cycle. If you don't do it right, your prospect may feel as you did sitting with your eyes closed on the examination table. Successful probing takes place when the prospect feels comfortable with you and is willing to share information that will reveal his or her needs and wants. The technique that is used in probing is simply to ask open-ended questions—who, what, how, when and why—that are designed to uncover facts, feelings, and attitudes about a specific topic. These questions allow prospects to respond as they please, which often uncovers information you wouldn't have asked about. There are many different types of probing questions. Figure 7–2 lists examples of types of open-ended questions that you will want to get comfortable with. Think of others that you can add to your own list.

The opposite of open-ended probing questions are closed-ended questions. These usually require a simple yes or no answer, or they require only the information specifically requested. For example, you ask the prospect, "What types of computers do you have?" The prospect replies, "All of our people are using 486s." In this example, you got exactly what you asked for. If you would have asked an open-ended question, such as, "How happy are you with your computers?" you might have gotten an ear full. Closed-ended questions are important. They help you better define problems and goals. They also help you control the conversation and move your agenda forward. Close ended questions are an excellent way to take control of a conversation. By asking a yes or no question, you are able to stop the conversation and then take it in the direction you want to go.

FIGURE 7–2
Types of Open-Ended Probing Questions

Type	Sample Question
1. Priorities	What is your time frame for completion?
2. Results	How do you plan to proceed?
	What are your goals for the coming year?
3. Opinions	Why do you want to make a change?
4. Basic	Who will be involved in the decision?
	What types of reports do you get?
	What do you need to run your business effectively?
5. Effects	What would happen if we changed the procedure?
6. Background	Could you tell me what kind of presses you are using?
	Your company sure produces an interesting product. How did you first think of it?
7. Confirmation	How interested are you in reaching this goal?
8. General	Have you lived (worked) in this area for a long time?
	How has your business changed over the past five years?

PROBING YOUR WAY TO SUCCESSFUL SALES

Let's look at some common remarks that a prospect might make to you during an initial sales call. The prospect might say, "I've been thinking about what I need to do, and I don't know if I'm ready to make a decision right now." You in turn could respond with, "Can you tell me why?" In this scenario, you are encouraging the prospect to expand upon what she just said. Or you could respond, "I can understand your decision not to move forward at this time. When do you think you would be ready to decide?" Or you could ask, "Is there anything that I can provide you in order for you to make a decision?" "Are you lacking information that you need to make a good decision?" As you can see, there are many ways that a conversation can go. That's why it is so important to always be listening to the prospect and reading his or her emotional and physical signals.

Let's look at this example: The prospect, an owner of a small graphic design shops says, "Our computers seem to be broken more often than our competitors'. This really causes a problem for us." Your response could be, "What seems to be the problem with them?" Or, if you thought for a moment, you would have realized that there could be several problems: The computers break down frequently, and because of this, there could be delivery problems, quality of work problems, and so on. Or maybe these computers are used night and day but were not meant to withstand such heavy usage. You will need to ask several different questions to find out the real problem.

In each of the above examples, you are trying to further uncover or clarify the prospect's true needs. By probing, you are asking the prospect to openly reveal her or his needs to you. By doing this, you will find out exactly what the prospect is looking for, what the prospect is trying to accomplish, what the prospect would like his or her equipment to do, and other needs and concerns that the prospect may have. Sometimes, prospects don't yet know if they have a need to satisfy. By using a closed probe, you can quickly learn to identify whether or not a real need exists. The following example will serve to clarify this point. You are attending the monthly meeting of the local contractor trade association and meet the president of a small contracting company. During the course of your conversation, he says,"Every day, I get at least two computer salespeople trying to sell me a new integrated system so I can keep track of my change orders and tie everything into one system." You really don't know if this person has a genuine need or if he is merely making a comment. To determine if a real need exists, you could try using a closed-probe question such as,"Is this really a problem in your business?" or, "If I'm hearing you correctly, you are looking for a way to better track your change orders."

The prospect will either reply: "Oh, no. It's not a problem" or "Yea, I wish I could solve this problem." If the response is the latter, you will need to switch to some open probes so you can find out more about the problem. Probing is a crucial part of the fact-finding process. As you probe deeper, the prospect will often come back with objections. In Chapter 9, we will teach you how to overcome any objection that a prospect or existing client may throw at you.

Remember these key words when constructing an open-ended probing question: who, what, when, where, and how. Start a question with one of these words, and you are on your way to asking a probing question. There are numerous benefits of good questioning. If you know how to effectively use questions, you will be able to do the following:

1. More precisely identify the prospect's true needs.

2. Increase your ability to match your services to the prospect's needs.

3. Demonstrate your expertise as a problem solver for the prospect.

4. Develop rapport with the prospect.

5. Find out more background information about the company than your competitors.

6. Confirm information you already know from your preparation for the meeting.

7. Close more business and grow your practice's top and bottom line.

Now that you know how to probe, we are going to show you how to sell benefits. As they say on Madison Avenue, "Don't sell the bacon; sell the sizzle."

Chapter Eight

Sell the Sizzle, Not the Bacon: How to Make Effective Presentations

INTRODUCTION

Asking for the business is the logical culmination of the consultative sales process. But to get to that stage, you will have to go through the entire sales cycle. If you try to shortcut the process, you won't be successful. At this point in the process, you have determined the prospect's needs and a way to provide the necessary benefits. Now you must help the client make the right buying decision. To do that, you must show the prospect that a particular service or product will satisfy his or her needs. In other words, the prospect will get the benefits that he or she is looking for. Benefit presentation is a key outcome of the fact-finding meeting.

SELF-ASSESSMENT 8–1: PRESENTATION SKILLS

This assessment will show you what you need to know about presentations. Answer each question with a yes or no.

1. I can readily explain the difference among a service feature, benefit, and value to a prospect.
2. The most important part of any presentation is telling the prospect about your services.
3. As a professional services firm, we don't need evidence about what we do.
4. Our written proposals are all the same; we just change the name and the price.
5. We seldom prepare for oral presentations.

(Answers: You should have answered question 1 yes, and 2–5 no.)

SELL THE SIZZLE

When you conceptualize the service from the prospect's point of view, your sales message is much more powerful. Keep in mind that there are distinct differences between service features, benefits, and value, though all are important.

Features: These are characteristics or facts about your service. Each service usually has several features, each of which may represent a solution or benefit to a specific problem. For example, you have fully automated your tax processing and you have fully trained tax preparers and reviewers. Or you belong to a regional firm and you have 15 offices throughout a four-state region.

Benefits: This is the worth received from a specific service feature. Benefits answer the question: "What's in it for me?"

In *Selling Without Confrontation,* Jack Greening lists several key ideas about benefits:

- Benefits are the only things you have to sell.
- A benefit is something tangible that the client receives.
- Action verbs tell the listener that something is a benefit:
  - Increase, expand.
  - Define, improve.
  - Decrease, delete, eliminate, save, reduce.
- Benefits can be used in statement or question form.
- Benefits can appeal to logic.
- Benefits can appeal to emotion.
- Benefits can be long- or short-term.
- Benefits can be to a customer's customers as well as to the customer.

Value: When a benefit is related to an expressed need, value is derived. The prospect must understand the value before he or she will make a commitment. Never assume that a prospect can figure out what the benefits are. Whenever you are discussing features and benefits, always relate them to the ultimate value the prospect will receive. Here's an example of how to apply this principle:

Service: Tax planning.

Feature: "Through tax planning, we can lay out alternative accounting methods and determine the tax and financial implications of each."

Benefit: "This service gives you a solid base on which to build business decisions, not only for current operations, but for the future."

Stated
Value: "A comprehensive tax service extends beyond standard compliance work. Tax planning anticipates the future growth of your company and is essential to your success."

EVIDENCE

To reinforce your sales message, you need evidence of the value of the services you are selling. If you are selling tax planning services, to use the previous example, you can show the prospect an actual case in which money was saved or better business planning resulted. Selling an audit service? Show prospects examples of clear, concise financial statements using graphs, pie, and bar charts and management comment reports that offer money-saving ideas. Other forms of evidence include references, time schedules for completing the project, testimonials, and client surveys. We are frequently amazed at how few CPAs actually have testimonial letters from existing clients. It is true that clients will seldom write these letters out of the blue. What you need to do is draft the letter for the client, ask them to make any changes, and have it prepared on their letterhead. These testimonial letters may be the most powerful sales tool you ever have.

The next most powerful tool is the use of presentation aides. Whenever possible, use graphs, handouts, overhead transparencies, poster boards, videos, statistics, flow charts, slides, and so on. And if you really want to move into the 21st century, use one of the newer computer-generated slide presentation programs. You may be asking yourself, Why bother? The answer is simple. We live in a visual society, and these visual aids help reinforce your message, aid retention, and support active listening. Studies have shown that we retain only 10 percent of what we hear, about 20 percent of what we see, and 60 percent of what we see and hear. If you want your prospects to have a lasting memory of you and your firm, you need to show and tell what you can do for them. The majority of what we learn comes from seeing something (about 82 percent), 11 percent of our learning experiences come from hearing something, and the remaining learning experiences come from smell (4 percent), touch (2 percent), and taste (1 percent). Therefore, if you want your clients to remember and learn something from your presentation, use visuals.

Example 8–1 provides you with an easy way to get your thoughts down on paper. It will help you become aware of the benefits that your services provide. To get you started, we recommend that you list all your services and other firm features and then develop your benefits list. Also, fill in the different types of evidence you currently have. If the evidence column is fairly empty, you will have a lot of work to do. Not having physical evidence or proof of what you say you can do is a major barrier to being a successful business developer.

EXAMPLE 8–1
Features Benefits and Evidence

1. **Service Feature:** Operational Review
2. **Benefits to Prospect:** Highlight areas for improvement; firm will run more efficiently, reduce overhead expenses, and so on.
3. **Evidence:** We have performed this service for 10 clients, we have articles written in the local press and have several testimonial letters verifying the results.

You should complete the above information for each one of your services and service areas. This information should be shared with all your staff. Since this information is of a general nature—in other words, it does not relate to a specific prospect or client ned—you will need to go through one more exercise. Exercise 8–2 helps you tie your features, benefits, and evidence to your prospect's needs. Use the following format to plan the best way to communicate your firm's solutions to a prospect.

EXERCISE 8–2

1. Identify one of your prospect's needs.
2. Describe your firm's ability to satisfy that need.
3. Outline the benefits that relate to the above ability.
4. Illustrate your ability to deliver the benefit—that is, the evidence.

Let's take an example. In this case, the prospect's need is to better manage his overhead; you feel that by conducting an operational review you can best meet and satisfy this need. This is your service solution. There will be many benefits to the client. One, you will highlight specific operational areas for revenue improvement and overhead reduction; two, the firm will run more efficiently; three, it will be more profitable; and so on. Your evidence will be testimonial letters, articles you have written about the operational review process, and so on.

PRESENTATIONS

You can use the above technique for making oral presentations and for written proposal presentations. Most of us don't have to prepare a formal proposal when we are dealing with smaller clients. Nevertheless, the presentation of the benefits is crucial to the success of your sales effort. This presentation, whether written or verbal, is your tangible effort as a consultant to partner with the prospect in order to fill his or her needs. Because of your knowledge about the prospect's needs and decision-making process, you are now able to present the best solution. Your presentation is really how you will solve the prospect's problems and needs by providing certain benefits. Too often at this stage, accountants begin to describe their firm and their services, which is a features-oriented rather than a benefits-oriented approach. They are not promoting the benefits of their services and the solutions that they bring to the table.

WRITTEN PROPOSALS

If the prospect asks you to mail in your proposal, firmly request the opportunity to present it in person. At the end of this chapter, we will give you some hints on how to make effective oral presentations. The personal presentation is a key in establishing your relationship in our consultative partnership approach and will allow you to handle objections, clarify questions, and physically ask for the business. A presentation by the person or team that will provide the service is more personal and more convincing than simply mailing in the proposal.

In her book *Winning Proposals,* published by the American Institute of Certified Public Accountants, pp. 27–28, Kaye Vivian offers 12 criteria that a prospect will use to evaluate you and your firm in a written proposal. Here are the 12 Cs that Vivian discusses:

Cost. Is your fee in the acceptable range?

Chemistry. Do we like and trust them and do they like and trust us?

Comparable experience. For whom have you handled similar issues?

Capabilities. Do you have the trained staff and technology on hand in the right locations?

Credentials. Who are your clients?

Clear communications. Do you tell us what we want/need to know as often as we would like and in the form we like?

Client service commitment. How important are we to them and what do their references say?

Centralized control. Can the service team members manage this work effectively and efficiently?

Competence. Can we rely on them to do the right thing?

Continuity. How will they limit staff turnover?

Creativity/initiative. Will they look for ideas/savings to bring to us?

Contacts. How well do we know members of the proposal team?

Of all of these criteria, Kaye Vivian identifies cost capabilities, chemistry, and comparable experience as key. Remember, your presentation is not a statement of qualifications or a fee proposal, nor is it an engagement letter that focuses on what you will do, who will be responsible, what the costs will be, and so on.

Developing the Written Proposal

The written proposal sets the stage and provides much of the actual contractual framework for your partnership with your prospective costumer. It is structured around needs analysis, benefits desired, and the link to the features your firm will provide through its products/services and people. When developing the proposal, you use your research and fact-finding to provide you with an understanding of the key benefits you must address. Proposals should consist of the following sections.

The Opening Letter (Executive Summary). Include a cover letter with your proposal. Take this opportunity to thank the prospect for the opportunity to propose your services. Unless your proposal is very brief, you also should briefly explain what the proposal will cover and how it is organized. A good executive summary should not be more than two pages. Many times, with shorter proposals, the entire proposal is often no more than a few pages. We feel that this is really more of a modified engagement letter, not a true proposal.

Description of Prospect's Needs. Here, you summarize what you learned about the prospect's concerns during your research and meetings. Be as specific as you can, using quantitative data concerning sales and financial performance where appropriate. Relate the service need to the organization's history and goals to clearly identify how your services will enable the prospect to move forward. For instance, suppose a growing business that has outstripped its current information system asks you to propose a new system. Your description could read as follows:

> A strong product line and excellent marketing have moved X Corp. to $5 million in sales in only three years. Research indicates that demand for your products remains strong and further potential for growth is excellent. Currently, however, X Corp. management is hampered by a lack of timely, reliable data due to outdated hardware and software in its MIS department. Without upgrading systems to meet current and projected future needs, X Corp. will be unable to adequately serve current customers or generate the information necessary to plan for future growth.

Our proposed systems upgrades will enable X Corp. to do the following:

- Accurately track sales to reduce billing errors and improve collections.
- Improve inventory tracking and management to reduce current inventory levels, eliminate stockouts, and decrease occurrences of obsolescence.
- Increase the timeliness, accuracy, and flexibility of X Corp.'s financial reporting system, giving management quick access to real-time financial data. Improved quality and usefulness of data will allow management to project and compare results to improve planning.

Statement of Objectives.   Be brief, direct, and clear when stating your firm's objectives. For simple engagements, you may need only one statement; more complicated engagements could require several. Initiate each statement with a strong action verb. Sample statements for our example could be as follows:

- Increase system storage capacity by 200 percent to meet current and projected needs.
- Improve reporting capabilities and simplify reporting procedures to enable management to effectively access and manipulate data.

Proposed Approach.   The next section is generally called the Proposed Approach, but many firms use terms such as the *System Solution* or the *ABC Approach*. You are explaining how you would go about solving the problem at hand. If it were an operational review engagement, a particular firm might call their approach the Best in Class Approach because they would be comparing the prospect's operating statistics with the best in the industry. This section describes the product or service you are proposing to satisfy the objectives above; it spells out specifically what you will do and how. It should relate each task to the client's needs, to your stated objectives, and to the resulting benefits. Remember your audience when describing tasks: Keep discussions on their level and focused on their reasons for buying the product or service. You will also want to provide as much identification of your competitive advantage as possible without direct reference to the competition.

Service Team and Responsibilities.   In this section, you introduce the professionals assigned to the engagement and briefly describe why they were selected. Don't give complete resumes; you can include them in the addenda. Spell out the roles and responsibilities of each team member.

Implementation and Costs.   Remember that the proposal is a legal offer. In this section, you will want to include the following information:

- Product/service specifications.
- Timing of when the work will be done.
- Fees and payment.

State your fee simply, including a list of all services provided. Avoid including hourly billing rates. It's best to give a fixed amount or open-ended quote. If the engagement is to be billed on an hourly basis, include an estimate of the number of hours required. Also include an implementation schedule and time fame.

The Final Step. Thank the prospect again for this opportunity and indicate your excitement. Finally, spell out the next step. For example, "Upon your agreement to this project, we will be ready to begin the engagement within 15 days."

Addenda. If appropriate, you may include a firm history, resumes of the engagement team, references, or promotional materials and articles. These are additions to, not part of, your proposal.

Packaging Your Proposal. A proposal is a marketing as well as contractual and sales tool. As such, its appearance, the quality of its writing, and the method of its presentation are critical. Each prospect has specific needs and specific reasons for considering your products/services. Each prospect deserves his or her own proposal. Avoid boilerplate, that is, canned paragraphs. If used at all, boilerplate should be confined to firm histories, product and service brochures, and resumes of service personnel.

Since your proposal is a marketing piece, consider its appearance. Does the quality of the paper and the cover reflect the importance of the piece? Are there opportunities within the proposal to use graphics? For instance, are there areas in which information could be conveyed more clearly by a chart or graph? Remember that a written proposal is one-way communication. It must set the stage for two-way communication in the presentation. It is not meant to take the place of any twoway communication that is vital for the selling process.

ORAL PRESENTATIONS

Arnold Palmer said, "The more I practice, the luckier I get." One thing that all authorities say is the key to a good presentation is to practice. Practice and critique yourself with a video tape if possible.

At the very least, practice in front of other members of your firm. Practice builds confidence. Confidence is contagious. Confidence makes you and your presentation a winner. Here are 12 suggestions for a successful presentation. Keep these handy the next time you have a presentation opportunity.

1. Practice what you plan to say using, a script.
2. Practice using your script and visual aids together so that you feel comfortable with the slides or overheads.
3. Now, reduce your script to notes. Just keep the key ideas you want to cover.
4. Now you are ready to practice without the script or visuals in case they get lost.
5. Present your presentation to colleagues and have them role-play the client audience.
6. Make sure your colleagues critique the presentation.
7. Time yourself. The last thing you want to do is go overtime and be cut off by the prospect.
8. Practice again.
9. When using slides or overheads, do not read from them. Speak to your audience not to the visual.
10. If you are going to use handouts, give them out at the beginning, number the pages, and guide your audience through them. Once the audience has a handout, their tendency will be to flip through it.
11. Make sure you can answer any question that may arise.
12. Finally, if something can go wrong, it will. Anticipate the unexpected.

HEADING TOWARD OBJECTIONS

Whether you've made your presentation to a crowded boardroom or to a single buyer/decision maker, your next task in the process is to handle objections. In fact, you want to turn objections into the basis for your close. Regardless of how well you develop your proposal and how well you made your oral presentation, there will generally be questions and objections. Remember that asking for the business and closing the business are processes that depend on two-way communication, not just a slick presentation. In fact, an absence of questions and objections may be the worst thing that can happen since you will not be able to detect any positive buying cues from the prospect.

In the next chapter, we will show you how to overcome objections you will certainly field in any selling situation.

Chapter Nine

Overcoming Objections

INTRODUCTION

In a recent issue of *Personal Selling Power,* Jim Slavish wrote the following anecdote:

Not the Cheapest, Just the Best: A Short, Sweet Sale

About two years ago, I received a call from a potential customer asking for a price quote for insurance. He wanted me to give it to him right over the phone. He said he was calling around and had about five quotes and was looking to buy the cheapest he could get.

We're generally not looking for this type of customer since they'll probably be shopping again in six months. While I was getting the quotation form, I asked him a few questions about the car and its usage. I then asked him what he did for a living. Sometimes this can tell you about usage, too.

He said he worked for a gourmet chocolate company. I said, "That's amazing. I had no idea you folks had the cheapest chocolate in town." He said, "We're not the cheapest." I said, "Then why would anybody buy it?" He said, "Because we're the best in town." I said. "We're the best insurance agency in town, too." He said, "Okay, I see what you mean. I'll see you Monday morning,"—and he did.[1]

SELF-ASSESSMENT 9–1: UNDERSTANDING OBJECTIONS

Answer the following questions true or false. This assessment is meant to measure your understanding of objections and your attitudes toward them.

1. Prospects have objections because they just don't want to buy from us. True or false?

---

[1]*Personal Selling Power,* Vol. 13, No. 7, (October, 1993), p 71.

2. Once I get my price low enough, I know there won't be any further objections. True or false?
3. Every time prospects hand me an objection, I convince them they are wrong. True or false?
4. I recognize that an objection is the prospect's way of saying, "I'm not totally comfortable with your solution to my problem." True or false?
5. I will always try to answer the objection as soon as it is presented. True or false?
6. I follow a specific structure for answering objections. True or false?

(Answers: 1 F, 2 F, 3 F, 4 T, 5 F, 6 T. If your answers differed from these, you will need to read and understand the concepts we present in this chapter.)

HANDLING OBJECTIONS

When a prospect throws out an objection, he or she is merely telling you there is a question or doubt in his or her mind that still needs to be answered. It could be a fear from a past experience; it could be a doubt about your ability to solve the problem. Perhaps, you just didn't probe enough, or you tried to close the sales without really developing a relationship with the prospect. Handling objections is the natural outcome of probing. Once you have probed, you will know what to say to the prospect. When revealing your solutions, remember to stress the benefits. It's not the service that a prospect buys and wants. It's the benefits that the service will provide to the prospect. Prospects really don't care about the estate plan; what they care about is preserving their estate, providing security for their spouse, paying the least amount in estate taxes. These are some of the benefits that a good estate plan will provide.

Handling objections is really putting the *CPA* method of selling to work. In other words, you are seeking a consultative relationship with the prospect as a true business partner; you use consultative selling skills and techniques to solve their problems, and you embrace a sales orientation as part of your business and professional role. Your ultimate goal is a win-win solution. The biggest mistake you can make is to not prepare to handle objections. When we tell accountants they will have to prepare for objections, they often look at us with a strange glaze. Many years ago, we learned from an astute telemarketer a technique that is often used when making telephone calls. Before the salesperson was allowed to get on the phone, he or she would write out at the bottom of a 3 × 5″ index card an objection the prospect would most likely raise. Then, on each card, the salesperson would write out the response to the objection. This way, the salesperson would never be caught off guard. All the cards were then put into plastic holders and kept in a three-ring binder. As soon as the salesperson heard the objection, he or she could flip to the appropriate card and respond. Figure 9–1 shows a typical card.

We suggest this same technique for accountants. Remember: It's wise to be prepared for some common objections in advance of the initial call.

FIVE WAYS TO HANDLE OBJECTIONS

When faced with an objection, you can consider handling it in one of five ways. It's important to remember that you do not want to argue or confront the prospect with your response. Our CPA method of selling is a partnership in which both partners win.

1. **Agree with the objection.** Then try to qualify it or explain it. For example, you might want to start your reply as follows:
   - You are correct to say that. We are one of the smallest firms in the area, but let me explain why we have decided not to grow just for growth's sake.
   - That's right, we are the most expensive, but we are the best. Here's why.

   Psychologists know that when you agree with someone, you diffuse his or her ability to keep arguing.
2. **Don't answer the objection when presented.** In other words, tell the prospect you would be happy to address the issue but need to find out a few more details before you can give an accurate answer. The response that we often give our clients is, "If we could postpone talking about that for just a few minutes...." After having made this statement, you merely ask the prospect another question so that you can gain further information.
3. **Respond with a question.** To get further information about the objection that was just asked, ask another question. For example, the prospect says she is concerned that you also audit

FIGURE 9–1
Objection-Response Card

Response: The reason that our firm is small is that we specialize in working
with the small business owner. Our services are such that they require
experienced and mature professionals. We are selective about the
clients we accept.

Objection: Your firm is too small.

---

another company, which happens to be her competitor. You
might respond by saying. "You seem to be concerned about the
confidentiality of our relationship. Would you expand on that?
Or, "I'm not sure if I fully understand your concern. Would you
explain it in more detail?"

4. **Turn an objection into a positive selling point.** The client
   says to you, "Why should I hire a firm that has the highest fees
   in town?" You can respond, "Our fees are high because we have
   the best people in the profession. Most of our staff have
   advanced business degrees and more than eight years of
   experience. That means you will get a level of advice that most
   firms in this area cannot offer."

5. **Ask the prospect for his or her solution to the problem.** For
   example, "Tell me Mary, how would *you* like to approach this
   problem? Do you have any suggestions or ideas as to the best
   way to resolve the situation?" Many times, the prospect has
   given the issue a great deal of thought and has an outline of the
   solution in mind.

Now that you know ways to handle objections, we want to give you
a formal process for answering any objection. Figure 9–2 outlines the
step-by-step process.

TYPES OF OBJECTIONS

There are two primary types of objections: misunderstandings and
drawbacks.

FIGURE 9–2
Objection Handling Process

1. The minute you hear an objection: STOP AND LISTEN. (Remember all the techniques we taught you in Chapter 5.)
2. Make sure you have a clear understanding of what the objection is. Often, a prospect will string together several statements and objections.
3. If you don't have a crystal clear understanding, probe until you do. It is common for a prospect to throw out an objection that is not a real one or the primary one.
4. Make sure to acknowledge the objection. In other words, paraphrase the objection for the prospect.
5. Answer the real objection. Don't come back with an answer that does not address the objection. You will never get the sale if you do.
6. When you feel you have adequately answered the objection, ask the prospect the following question: "Are you satisfied with my response?" If the prospect says no, you will need to probe some more.

Source: Adapted from Charles Goldsmith, *Selling Skills for CPAs* (Englewood Cliffs, NJ: Prentice Hall, 1985), p. 118.

Misunderstandings

The prospect, because of lack of knowledge or misinformation about your firm or service, believes something that is not accurate. The prospect may have heard a rumor on the street about your firm or may have been told something false by a competitor or disgruntled employee. There are countless possibilities for misunderstandings, and that is why word-of-mouth advertising is so important; negative advertising can kill a firm. The more disgruntled clients and employees you have, the more they will be spreading stories about your firm in the market place. Since they are disgruntled, you can be sure the stories won't be positive.

Let's look at an example: The prospect objects to using your systems consulting group because he or she heard about an installation problem you had at another company. The prospect does not know that the problem was caused by faulty equipment and that it has been corrected to the satisfaction of the client. In this case, all you may have to do is explain the circumstances around the misunderstanding.

Let's look at another objection and how you might handle it regarding your **apparent** lack of experience in a prospect's industry.

Scenario:	The prospect believes you lack experience in his or her industry.
Prospect:	"I don't think you have enough experience in the health care field."
You:	"How important is our having experience in this industry to you?"
Prospect:	"It's pretty important since we compare our operating results to industry norms and adjust our pricing accordingly."
You:	"Most firms don't fully understand the scope of our experience in this industry. We may not have a significant number of clients. However, two of our larger clients are in this industry, and I think we can overcome your concern. Let me explain what we are currently doing. First, we are hiring an additional health care specialist next month. Second, we are sending one of our senior consultants to a six-week training program on operational procedures. Third..."

Drawbacks

Drawbacks are the more common type of objection. This type appears whenever you are unable to obtain a positive answer from question (6) (Are you satisfied with my response?) in Figure 9–2. The prospect is not satisfied with your response. This is not necessarily a negative. For example, a prospect is objecting to your final price quote and tells you that he is not going to use your service because of its costs. You have priced your services at rock bottom and cannot go any lower. If that is the case, it may be in your best interest just to say no to the prospect. This is clearly not a win-win situation.

Most of the time, you will want to minimize the importance of the objection by making the client aware of the benefits of your services. You should be able to demonstrate that the benefits will outweigh the drawback the client has voiced. Let's look at another solution to the cost issue.

Scenario:	The prospect objects to the cost of your service, and you cannot cut the price.
Prospect:	"I'd love to have this estate plan done, but $2,500 is more than my wife and I wanted to pay."
You:	"Let's take a minute and look at your needs in this area. You agreed that the plan meets your needs to distribute your estate equally to your spouse and heirs."

Prospect: "Yes, that's correct."

You: "You also agreed that it will take a lot of mental pressure off of you, knowing that the plan and trusts are in place."

Prospect: "Yes, that is very important for me. But I still can't afford to do this. Is there a way to do it for less?"

You: "There are some options we could explore. We could just do the first part of the plan. If you feel satisfied with our work, we would continue. But you would only be responsible for $1,000."

Or

"You know, it seems we are really focusing in on the cost side. Our plan will actually save you more than $150,000 in estate taxes and also save on some current federal and state taxes. The fee for the plan represents less than 2 percent of the total savings. Wouldn't you agree that the fee is worth it?"

If at this point in the conversation you feel the objection has been diffused, just sit tight. There is an old expression among salespeople that whenever you are in a situation like this "the first one to speak loses." You have thrown the ball back to the prospect; let him or her respond. If you speak too soon, you will have to give another reason to overcome the objection. If you wait for the prospect to respond and if the response is positive, you can move on to asking for the business.

THE TEN MOST OFTEN HEARD OBJECTIONS

The following are the most common objections you will face. You have probably heard most of them and have responded in one way or other. What is important about these objections is not what they say on the surface but what the prospect is actually saying to you. We have interpreted what prospects are saying when they make these statements.

1. **Your firm is too large.** There are several variations to this objection. For example: "We're just a small business. We don't need sophisticated advisors." No matter how this objection comes across, what the prospect is really saying is that she is afraid that because of your size, you won't pay enough attention to the business. This is the real issue you will have to overcome.

2. **Your firm is too small.** This is just the opposite of the above objection. Here the prospect is quietly telling you he is afraid you don't have the expertise to solve the problem. Or if it is a bigger client you are trying to obtain, the decision maker may be telling you that he can't afford to make a mistake by hiring a small firm without a national reputation. What would happen to him if the engagement went wrong and he would have to justify to his superiors the reason for taking a no-name firm over one of the national firms? Sometimes there will be objections that you will never be able to overcome. This particular one may be one of them. That's okay, just go on to the next prospect.

3. **Your fees are too high.** This is really a value objection. The prospect is not convinced that what she will get is worth the price you are charging. Your objective will be to demonstrate the value, the payback, how you have saved other clients significant dollars when performing the same services.

4. **We are satisfied with our current accountant.** This is probably the most often heard objection. A variation is, "I've been with so and so for 10 years. Why would I want to change?" There is no doubt that when someone is in a happy situation they most likely won't change. You can take the following approach when this objection arises. First, you can gain some competitive information. Merely ask the prospect why he is so happy with his accountant. Second, you can try to find out what the current accountant is not doing for the client. As the prospect begins to tell you all the things that the current accountant is doing, keep probing to see if there aren't some major gaps. You might also ask the client to give you an opportunity to review his tax return, just in case something was missed. This second opinion approach has worked successfully for many firms.

5. **You don't have expertise in my industry.** We have found that the prospect is really saying she is afraid they will be spending a lot of time training you and your people. In other words, the prospect feels you don't understand their industry or business operations. You need to determine if this is a drawback objection or a misunderstanding.

6. **You are too far away.** The prospect may be saying that they need someone who lives close by. But that might not be the real problem. Perhaps the prospect had a problem with poor

service in the past. This is what he is really telling you. How prompt will you be when there is a question or a problem that needs to be resolved? It's not a matter of physical distance but of time and responsiveness.

7. **It's too late in the year to change.** How often have you heard a prospect tell you to "call us next year"? In this objection, the prospect is really telling you she is concerned about the disruption that will occur if they change accountants now. You will need to present your transition timetable to make the prospect feel more comfortable with the change.

8. **We don't know your firm.** The client is looking for references. Perhaps your firm has a low profile and the prospect just doesn't have much to make a decision on. If this is a misunderstanding objection, you would show the prospect your involvement in the community; explain to him that your firm has been in existence since 1945 and has a high profile in the other section of town. You are now beginning to market in this area of the town, and so on.

9. **Let me think about it some more.** Either one of two things is going on here. One, the prospect just can't make a decision. We all know procrastinators. Two, you have not done a good job of probing or listening to the prospect. This is the prospect's way of telling you that. You either need to go back to the probing cycle or try to continue the relationship with the prospect by setting up another meeting.

10. **Who is really going to handle my account?** Here the prospect is telling you she is worried about the other people in your firm. Perhaps she hasn't met them yet. Word on the street may be that you are a great "up-front" person but that the clients never see you again. As with any other objection, you will need to respond to this one to the prospect's satisfaction if you want to get a new engagement.

There is no one correct response to these objections. But each firm should have somewhat of a consistent response so that all of your people are giving out the same message. Remember that you are providing solutions to your prospects and clients. You are not at war with them. Keep these points in mind:

1. Never argue with a prospect. There will be only one loser: you.

2. Always acknowledge the prospect's concerns and assure the prospect that you realize how important he or she is.

3. Address objections one at a time. If the prospect gives you several objections at one time, resolve one before going on to

the next one. An effective way of handling multiple objections is to write them out on a sheet of paper or flip chart. Then you can check them off as you answer them. After you have done this, it will be hard for the prospect to return to any of the previous objections she gave you.

4. Even if you can't do business with the prospect, let him know you want to help. If he should decide not to use you, you will be happy to recommend someone who can better solve her problem.

MOVING ON TO THE CLOSE

Okay. The meeting has gone well. You've built credibility and rapport with the prospective client, you've gathered specific information through probing questions and active listening, and you know what the company's needs are. You feel you've overcome all of the known objections. Now what? You can proceed to one of two steps:

1. Begin the process of closing the deal.
2. Open the door to the next visit.

If it is unlikely that you can proceed to the closing at the initial sales call, you must keep the door open. Your objective is to warmly indicate your firm's desire to work with the company and clearly establish a definite next step. You will want to indicate a date when they can expect your proposal and, if possible, set up a second meeting to discuss your firm's solutions to the company's problems or needs. Plan to leave the meeting with something: either a future appointment or a request for a proposal. The follow-up after a presentation is much too important for any professional to neglect. Any commitment you have made must be taken care of promptly so you can get back to your prospective client. A good follow-up tool is a letter that reinforces the prospect's recall of the following:

- The needs that you identified at the meeting
- The benefits to be derived from selecting your firm.
- A review of action steps by both your firm and the prospect.
- Any agreed-upon conclusions, necessary follow-up, and so on.

Don't forget, keep asking yourself how you can put to use today what you are reading in this book. In the next chapter, we'll tell you how to ask for the business.

Chapter Ten

Don't Leave without Asking for the Business

INTRODUCTION

You've designed solutions to the prospect company's needs. You've answered all of the objections that were thrown at you. You've developed the partner relationship with the prospect. Now there is only one more thing to do. Ask for the business. Ask the prospect for a commitment. You are going to close the sale.

This is a very serious step in the Consultative Partnership Approach. You must be confident and assertive, but you must not be overly aggressive or do anything to betray the trust with the prospect that you have so carefully cultivated. Your confidence and assertiveness is based on your assurance that your product and service is the best possible solution for the prospect. You have satisfactorily handled all objections. Now you need something from the prospect. You need their commitment.

SELF-ASSESSMENT 10–1: CLOSING SKILLS AND TECHNIQUES

Answer the following questions true or false. They will give you some idea of your knowledge about closing techniques and skills.

1. Selling and closing the sale is a continuous process.
2. A no from a prospect is a personal rejection.
3. I need to memorize at least 10 selling techniques to be effective.
4. The time to close is when the prospect is ready to buy.
5. My attitude will have an impact on the number of closes I can make.

(Answers: 1-T, 2-F, 3-F, 4-T, 5-T.)

WHY PROSPECTS DON'T SAY YES

You Didn't Ask!

A major problem for nonprofessional salespeople is simply asking for the business. Don't be afraid to ask for the order. Most sales are lost because the salesperson did not say, "When can we start?" Why are we afraid to ask? We perceive a no as a personal rejection, which is emotionally painful. After we have developed a personal relationship with the client, we don't want to lose face through rejection. So we simply don't ask for the business.

To be successful at selling, you must not consider a no a personal rejection. It simply means that your presented benefits did not meet the prospect's needs at this time or that there is an alternative that seems better than your offer. Perhaps you are simply too expensive for the prospect. Remember that every customer has a different view of value and may simply not be willing to pay for the best. As you now know, our consultative partnership approach does not view a no as final but simply as part of the continuing relationship-development process.

Change Is Difficult

Let's face it, there is a natural reluctance to change. Perhaps human nature follows Newton's law: A body at rest will tend to remain at rest, and a body in motion will tend to remain in motion, unless acted upon by an outside force. Your job is to be that force. To accept your offer, other offers must be rejected or old relationships with other accountants modified. The client may have to change systems or retrain personnel. Remember that your job is not to overpower the prospect but simply to make it easier for the prospect to say yes than no.

Any Decision Is Fear Producing

Our fear of making a bad decision is much worse than our fear of making no decision at all. If we make no decision, at least we know what will happen: business as usual. However, if we make a decision, things will change and we don't know how. Part of the closing process is to use the credibility you have built up with the prospect to reduce that fear so that he or she understands what will change and how it will change. In other words, you need to give the prospect a comfort level to accept the unknown.

You Didn't Let Them Say Yes!

That's right, many salespeople simply continue trying to "persuade" long after it's unnecessary and counterproductive. You have to know when to be quiet and let the prospect buy. To be successful, you need to be able to identify buying signals, which may be both verbal and non-verbal. These buying cues were discussed in detail in Chapters 5 and 6. You should recall that this is part of the active listening skills we discussed. This really isn't as difficult as you might think. Remember the prospect knows you are there to make a sale and she probably would not be taking the time to listen to you if she did not have a recognizable need and were not interested in your proposal.

CLOSING TECHNIQUES TO HELP THE PROSPECT SAY YES

It's time to ask for the business. Be direct; don't beat around the bush. Closing techniques should not be viewed as tricks to sell the prospect something she or he doesn't need. Rather, they are means of helping a friend make a right decision. There are many different ways to close a sale. Which one works? Well, they all do—sometimes. What we mean is that closing in the *CPA* method to selling should be the logical outcome of the process. Will it always work? Of course not. Is there a special technique you can use? Not really. You just need to be able to read the buying signals prospects send. Let's look at some examples that will help you close more business.

Prospect Cue Close

In the prospect cue close, the prospect is telling you that he or she is ready to do business. The prospect might say, "When can you start?" or "As we begin working on this project..." Or you might notice that the prospect begins to relax; this is usually a sign that a decision has been made to select you. Eyes may widen and arms open up; the client becomes warmer. If you notice any of these signals, it's time to ask for the business. The best signal in the world for accountants is when the prospect begins to complain about the service he or she is receiving from the present accountant. If you ever hear, "My current accountant seems to always be late in delivering my tax return" or, "You'll probably be just like my current accountant," make sure you find out why the prospect is saying these things and zero in on how you are different. Another key cue is when the prospect begins to talk about the fees he or she is currently paying. She may be telling you she doesn't think she is getting sufficient value for the fees. You need to show her the value she would get by hiring you. Again, this is your opportunity to strike and go for the close.

The Agreement Ladder Close

With this technique, initially you are trying to get prospects to agree to small points. As they agree to each point, your goal is to move them toward the close. You will be moving them from a simple to a more complex yes answer. The final question is a request for the sale. After you have done the probing and addressed all the objections, you might want to prioritize the objections, starting with the least significant. Review each objection and resolution with the prospect to get her or him to agree and then end with the close question: "What's stopping us from beginning this project?"

The following example should serve to clarify this approach. You may start off by asking the prospect, "Do you agree that this project is just what you need in order to turn your business around?" This is the first rung on the ladder. After the prospect agrees, you ask the next question, "Is the price I quoted in the range that you were looking for?" The next question could be "And the timing of the project fits your needs?" Each questions moves the prospect closer to the final question, "When do we start?" or "What's stopping us from beginning this project?"

The Impending Event Close

Sometimes fear of a threat can close the sale. This happens every day in retail sales. For example, you pick up the daily paper, and the ad shouts out, "Suits reduced from $499 to $299. One Day Only!" What the ad is really saying is that if you don't act now you will be penalized because you will pay $200 more after the sale ends. Now, we know accountants don't advertise sales such as these, but there are many impending events you can mention to prospects. Tell the prospect that unless they act now, the following might happen:

- Fees may increase.
- A tax increase or penalty may go into effect.
- A key staff member may not be available (either you or another key person) for the engagement.
- Your specialist is booked for the next two months and only has the next four days open to work on this project.
- There are several other pending projects that will begin shortly, and once they do you won't be able to get to this project for at least three months.

The Trial Close

Perhaps the most common type of closing technique is the trial close. It is something you should become adept at. The trial close comes closes to the old ABC (always be closing). If used correctly, it can take the pulse of your prospects. The purpose of this technique is to determine how ready the buyer is to say yes. Here are some examples of trial close questions:

- "How would you feel if we could begin this project next week?"
- "Do you think our approach will help you solve the problem?"
- "Do you feel comfortable working with a firm like ours?"
- "If I could free up my schedule to work with you, would you agree to our proposal?"
- "When would you want us to start?"

The important thing in trial close questions is that you give the prospect the opportunity to express his or her feelings and opinions about the project, your firm, the services suggested, and so on. When you ask these questions, the prospect might give you a negative answer (especially if you have not been following our suggested *CPA* selling method). More than likely, you will get a positive or qualified positive answer to the trial close question. For example, "If you could get started next week, that would be great. However, I am concerned about the fees." If you get a qualified answer like this one, identify the objection, try to overcome it, and then go back with another trial close question.

With all of the above techniques, it is important to ultimately ask for the order. If you follow our suggestions, you won't have to memorize any of the traditional closing approaches. (And believe us, there are many that we never mentioned here.) In our Consultative Partnership Approach to selling, you are never forcing prospects to use a service or buy a product that is not right for them. As we saw earlier, a key element of successful sales is attitude. Always expect a positive response from your prospects; once the prospect says yes, stop closing and say just one more word: "Congratulations!"

The next chapter presents what we consider to be the top 10 secrets to successful business development as well as a method of managing your own behavior. These secrets and the goal-setting process will further help you put into practice the ideas you have learned in this book.

Chapter Eleven

Ten Secrets of Success:

How to Manage Your Own Behavior to Become Sales Oriented

INTRODUCTION

Congratulations! You have completed the Consultative Partnership Approach to selling accounting services. There is just one more thing you have to do: Put what you've learned into practice.

This chapter contains not only the secrets of being successful at sales, the phrases and affirmations you should jot down and keep with you when the going gets rough, but also a process to make sure you are successful: the goal-setting process. Part of being successful in sales or in anything else is having a clear vision of what you want to accomplish. The other part is the constant reinforcement of positive statements that you are a successful and worthwhile individual. At the end of this chapter, we have included a personal business development plan overview form for you to complete.

SELF-ASSESSMENT 11–1: GOAL SETTING

1. I keep score of the new business I bring in on a weekly basis. True or false?
2. All the professional staff in my firm have personal business development plans: written goals for new business. True or false?
3. On an annual basis, all our professionals complete a written goal-setting plan. True or false?
4. We meet on a monthly basis to review our marketing and selling success and activity. True or false?

(Answers: You should have answered each question true.)

SETTING GOALS

Setting and achieving effective and measurable goals for both firm and individual marketing will be the key to your success. Goals are defined as having five key characteristics. An easy way to remember them is to think of the word SMART:

Specific. The goal is targeted and has an understandable and clearly defined objective.

Measurable. The goal has a specific deadline, and results can be quantified.

Attainable. Deals with events and forces that are within you or your firm. You must have or be able to get the resources to achieve the goal.

Realistic. Deals with aspects that are outside of you and your firm. Within your enviroment, make sure you can accomplish that goal. In other words, there are no known external forces which will stop you or your firm.

Tangible. The goal can be easily visualized by the person who is to accomplished it. If you can't visualize it or dream it, you surely won't be able to accomplish it.

The question becomes "How do we apply this concept to developing SMART marketing goals?" The best way we can illustrate is by example.

Let's assume that your firm is planning to target automobile dealerships. At first blush, you might define a SMART goal as the following: From now until December 31, 19XX, we want to develop $150,000 in business from the automotive industry. Unfortunately, this statement is far from where we need to be in developing a truly SMART goal. To develop a SMART goal, an ultimately effective goal, you must ask the following questions:

- How many new clients will it take to reach the $150,000 goal?
- Is there a target for realization or profitability in achieving that goal?
- Will this volume goal come from new clients or expansion of service to existing clients?
- Will we allocate the necessary resources to achieve this goal and budget the appropriate marketing time and dollars toward advertising, promotion, practice development, and so on?
- Do you possess the necessary talent, whether it be in the form of technical or marketing abilities, to either create the lead or participate in closing the sale?

At this point, most of us might feel comfortable that we have in fact a SMART goal. Right? Wrong! The real work is only beginning. We call this the action plan. If we know we need $150,000 of business and know that the average client fee is $10,000, this tells us that we need 15 clients. However, to obtain 15 clients, we know we need to get in front of 60 prospects, as our close ratio is 25 percent. However,one-third of those people we get in front of don't even qualify as prospects, as they simply are meeting to gain information. Of those 80 prospects/information seekers that we meet with, we estimate that 20 percent of our appointments will forget to show up or cancel; thus we need 96 appointments just to meet face-to-face with 80 people.

To get to 96 potential appointments, we know we have to make three calls to each of those prospects, or 288 phone calls. We have found that it takes at least three attempts on the telephone to even get in touch with each of the 288 prospects. Thus, we conclude that we have to make 864 attempts on the phone just to get the 96 appointments we previously described.

If you really want to control your destiny, you probably want to break the 864 phone calls into 72 calls per month, 18 calls per week, or even more precisely, 3.6 calls per day. We realize that this method is totally foreign to most accountants. But if you can't measure your marketing activities, you won't be able to manage them. Just as there are many loopholes to choose from in the tax law, so are there loopholes in CPA firm marketing and selling activities. However, in marketing we want to close the loopholes. The type of process we have described above removes many of those loopholes and causes your marketing efforts to turn into solid results.

Many accountants initially have told us that the above menthod involves too much work and record keeping. Our response is that if you and your staff don't report on a monthly basis on how well each of you is doing, how will you know if you are on track? We also respond to their comment with a quote from Chuck Coonradt, who asked, "If winning isn't important, why do we spend all that money on scoreboards?" Chuck's question goes to the heart of implementation, which is by far the most difficult and important aspect of marketing. Far too often, the importance of implementation is lost in the planning of individual goals. We, as individuals and firms, need to commit ourselves both to SMART marketing planning and marketing implementation.

There is one more aspect of goal setting that you need to practice. Once you establish your goals, write down affirmations, positive statements about yourself and how you will feel when the goal is finally achieved.

Mike McCaffrey, in his seminar entitled FOCUS (Freedom of Choice & Understand Success) defines an affirmation as follows: "An affirmation describes what you want as opposed to what exists or what you don't want." (*FOCUS Seminar Handbook*, p. 16) Let's look at some affirmations:

- "I am a successful partner in a quality CPA firms that helps its clients become more successful."
- "I enjoy showing others in my firm how to bring in new business."
- "I am proud of the new business I can bring into my firm."

Finally, you need to write out your goals. Figure 11–1 can be used as a goal-planning form to help you put your goals down in writing. You should complete this form for each goal you set for yourself.Use Appendix 11–1 to capture your personal goals for the current or coming fiscal year.

FIGURE 11–1
Goal Planning Form

---

1. Write your SMART Goal here: _____
2. List the benefits to you and your firm when you achieve the above goal. How will you feel? Write these benefits out and keep them with you so that you can give yourself positive affirmations: _____
   _____
   _____
3. Outline the necessary action steps with target completion dates. _____
   _____
   _____
4. How will you keep score? _____

OUR 10 SECRETS FOR SUCCESS

We wish we could attribute the following concepts and statements to the professionals we first heard them from. However, over the years, we have heard and read them in a variety of sources. Most of them have been around a long time and have become part of our everyday language. If you set clearly defined goals and keep these secrets in mind, we are sure you will begin to see small successes that will only lead to larger ones. The little effort makes a world of difference when you look at it in terms of a week, a month, or a year.

Secret 1

Attitude

Attitude is everything. It determines everything: your happiness, your health, and your wealth.

Secret 2

Satisfaction Can Kill You

Don't be satisfied. If you are happy with the way things are, you are probably in a rut.

Secret 3

You Can't Coast Uphill

Coasting will only take you in one direction: downhill

Secret 4

Passion

Fire in the belly will take you a long way.

Secret 5

Results Count

Do what is important. Don't confuse activities with results.

Secret 6

Set Goals

Setting goals will get you to the top faster. If you don't have a plan or don't know where you are going, how will you ever know when you get there?

Secret 7

Know Your Product

Know your service and products better than anyone else. Know their benefits; that's what your prospects are buying.

Secret 8

Kiss a Lot

Keep It Simple, Sam or Sally! Don't talk jargon to your prospects or clients.

Secret 9

Don't Be Afraid to Dream

If you don't dream it, it won't happen.

Secret 10

Make the Most of Yourself

You are your most important asset.
Invest in yourself daily. Keep
growing so that you constantly
pay high dividends.

Appendix 11–1

PERSONAL GOALS AND ACTION PLANS

199X
Prepared by: _____
Date: _____
Department: _____
Office: _____
Department head: _____
Counselor: _____

PERSONAL BUSINESS DEVELOPMENT PLAN—OVERVIEW

PLAN YEAR

Name: Date:

SUMMARY GOALS:

	Current Year		Next Year	
	Hours	Dollars	Hours	Dollars
1. Hours/Dollars				
Billable				
Practice development				
2. Billing rate				
	Present	$	Future	$

3a. Current specialty area(s) of practice:

_____
_____
_____

3b. Goal for expansion of specialty area(s) in 199_:

_____
_____
_____

4. New business development goals:
   Number of new clients
   Fees generated for firm
      Present clients $
      New clients$
5. Referral base expansion goal:
      Number of referral sources generated
      Number of referral meetings per month
      Number of referrals from existing clients
6. Write-off percentage goal:
      A/R   WIP
         %   %

7. Firm management goals

   _____

   _____

8. Marketing activity goals (Develop written goals in each area using
   Figure 11–1 goal-planning form.)
       Creating public image
       Developing relationships
       Selling/closing
       Retaining clients
9. Professional education goals:

   _____

   _____

10. Other (administrative, intangible, for example, develop leadership skills,
    better judgment, self-esteem, etc.)

    _____

    _____

    _____

CONGRATULATIONS!

You should congratulate yourself. You have just finished the Consultative Partnership Approach to selling accounting services. All of us are ready to help you achieve your maximum potential. If you would like a personal consulting session, feel free to write or call any of us:

August J. Aquila, Ph.D.
4732 Chantrey Place
Minnetonka, MN 55345
612-930-1295

Allan D. Koltin, CPA
401 North Michigan Suite 2600
Chicago, IL. 61611
312-245-1940

Robert Pitts, Ph.D.
DePaul University
Department of Marketing
One East Jackson
Chicago, IL 60604
312-362-8109

Selected Readings

Alessandora, Anthony J. *Non-Manipulative Selling*. SanDiego, CA: Corseuvane, Inc., 1979

Alessandra, Anthony and Rick Barrera. *Collaborative Selling*, New York, NY: John Wiley and Sons, 1993.

Berry, Leonard L., Charles M. Futrell, and Michael R. Bowers. *Bankers Who Sell: Improving Selling Effectiveness in Banking*. Homewood, IL: Business One Irwin, 1985.

Connelly, J. Campbell. *A Manager's Guide to Speaking and Listening*. New York, NY: American Management Association, 1967.

Giovagnoli, Melissa, *Mega Networking*, Chicago, IL: Dearburn Financial Publishing, Inc, 1995.

Goldsmith, Charles. *Selling Skills for CPAs: How to Bring in New Business*. Englewood Cliffs, NJ: Prentice Hall, 1985.

Greening, Jack. *Selling Without Confrontation*. Binghampton, NY: Haworth Press, 1993.

Kotler, Philip and Paul N. Bloom. *Marketing Professional Services*. Englewood Cliffs, NJ: Prentice Hall, 1984.

McCaffery, Mike. *Freedom of Choice & Understanding Success*. Laguna Beach CA: Mike McCaffrey & Associates, Inc., 1992.

Marcus, Bruce W. *Competing for Clients in the 90s*, rev. ed. Chicago, IL: Probus, 1992.

Nassutti, Colette P. (Editor), T*he Marketing Advantage: How to Get and Keep the Clients You Want*. New York, NY: AICPA, 1994.

Oberhaus, Mary Ann, Sharon Ratliffe and Vernon Stauble, *Professional Selling: A Relationship Process*, Forth Worth, TX: Harcourt Brace College Publishers, 1993.

Peters, Tom. *Thriving on Chaos: Handbook for a Management Revolution*. New York, NY: Alfred A. Knopf, 1987.

Reid, David A. *The Sales Presentation Manual*. St. Paul, MN: West Publishing Company, 1992.

Strong, E.K., Jr. *The Psychology of Selling and Advertising*. New York, NY: McGraw Hill Book Company, 1925.

Vivian, Kaye. *Winning Proposals*. New York, NY: American Institute of Certified Public Accountants, 1993.

Wilson Learning Corporation. *The Versatile Salesperson Reference Handbook*. Eden Prairie, MN: Wilson Learning Corporation, 1985.

Index